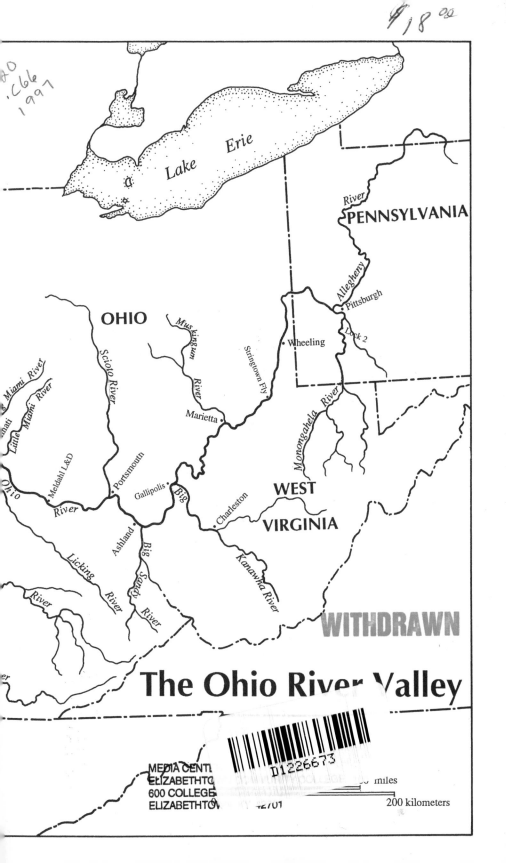

Lake Erie

PENNSYLVANIA

River

Allegheny

OHIO

Muskingum

Scioto River

River

Pittsburgh

Lock 2

Wheeling

Stringtown Fly

Little Miami River

Great Miami River

Cincinnati

Marietta

Meldahl L&D

Portsmouth

Gallipolis

Big

Ashland

Monongahela River

Charleston

WEST

VIRGINIA

Ohio

River

Licking

Big Sandy River

River

River

River

Kanawha River

The Ohio River Valley

miles

200 kilometers

THE OHIO RIVER VALLEY SERIES

Rita Kohn and William Lynwood Montell
Series Editors

LIFE ON
THE OHIO

Captain James Coomer

THE UNIVERSITY PRESS OF KENTUCKY

Publication of this volume was made possible in part
by a grant from the National Endowment for the Humanities.

Copyright © 1997 by The University Press of Kentucky

Scholarly publisher for the Commonwealth, serving
Bellarmine College, Berea College, Centre College of Kentucky,
Eastern Kentucky University, The Filson Club Historical Society,
Georgetown College, Kentucky Historical Society, Kentucky State
University, Morehead State University, Murray State University,
Northern Kentucky University, Transylvania University,
University of Kentucky, University of Louisville,
and Western Kentucky University.

Editorial and Sales Offices: The University Press of Kentucky
663 South Limestone Street, Lexington, Kentucky 40508-4008

01 00 99 98 97 5 4 3 2 1

Library of Congress Cataloging-in-Publication Data
Coomer, James, 1928-
   Life on the Ohio / James Coomer.
      p.   cm. — (The Ohio River Valley series)
   ISBN 0-8131-2000-4 (cloth : alk. paper)
      1. Ohio River—Social life and customs—Anecdotes. 2.Ohio
River—Description and travel—Anecdotes. 3. Coomer, James,
1928- —Anecdotes. 4. Ohio River—Biography—Anecdotes.
5. River steamers—Ohio River—Anecdotes. 6. River life—Ohio
River—Anecdotes. I. Title. II. Series.
F520.C66   1997
977'.033—dc21   97-14526

This book is printed on acid-free recycled paper
meeting the requirements of the American National Standard
for Permanence of Paper for Printed Library Materials.

Manufactured in the United States of America

"Nice? It's the only thing," said Water Rat to Mole. "Believe me, my young friend, there is nothing—absolutely nothing—half so much worth the doing as simply messing about in boats."

Kenneth Grahame, *Wind in the Willows*

To my children and grandchildren:
my son CAPTAIN JIM COOMER,
a fourth-generation river man
and father of SARAH ELIZABETH;
SUSAN KELLY, mother of BLOSSOM and ANDREW;
MELISSA BELLEN, mother of CAMILLE and ANDREA;
and JENNIFER, who died too young, the mother of DENINA.

Contents

CONTENTS

Illustrations

Series Foreword

The Ohio River Valley Series, conceived and published by the University Press of Kentucky, is an ongoing series of books that examine and illuminate the Ohio River and its tributaries, the lands drained by these streams, and the peoples who made this fertile and desirable area their place of residence, of refuge, of commerce and industry, of cultural development, and, ultimately, of engagement with American democracy. In doing this, the series builds upon an earlier project, "Always a River: The Ohio River and the American Experience," which was sponsored by the National Endowment for the Humanities and the humanities councils of Illinois, Indiana, Kentucky, Ohio, Pennsylvania, and West Virginia, with a mix of private and public organizations.

The Always a River project directed widespread public attention to the place of the Ohio River in the context of the larger American story. This series expands on this significant role of the river in the growth of the American nation by presenting the varied history and folklife of the region. Each book's story is told through men and women acting within their particular place and time. Each reveals the rich resources for the history of the Ohio River and of the nation afforded by records, papers, and oral stories preserved by families and institutions. Each traces the impact the river and the land have had on individuals and cultures and, conversely, the changes these individuals and cultures have wrought on the valley with the passage of years.

As a force of nature and as a waterway into the American heartland, the Ohio and its tributaries have touched us individually and collectively. This series celebrates the story of that river and its valley through multiple voices and visions. *Life on the Ohio* is Captain Jim Coomer's chronicle of his personal and profession odyssey as a third-generation pilot, the family calling now being continued by his son. Captain Coomer pays tribute to the unfairly neglected workhorse of the river, the harbor tug, whose land-based crews are on twenty-four-hour call to keep the ever-moving caravan of long-distance tows supplied, fueled, serviced, and repaired. Coomer also tells of life as seen from the pilothouse on the big boats, a principal mode of getting raw materials to their destinations that far outranks any other method of transportation in tonnage and economy. The Ohio River alone ships more cargo than the Panama Canal; the Ohio and the Mississippi move some 260 million tons a year; and Coomer has been there, a pilot and a captain on the towboats. He tells it like it is. If he's short on nostalgia, he's long on reality. If he's hard on himself, he's soft on the natural beauty of "La Belle Riviere." The Ohio is a working river, and Coomer is a working Ohio riverman. Rendered in his distinctive voice, *Life on the Ohio* illuminates one man's experiences from soon after World War II to the recent past and helps us understand a specialized industry without which, as a nation, we'd be economically endangered.

RITA KOHN
WILLIAM LYNWOOD MONTELL
Series Editors

Foreword

Of course, I'm partial to river themes. I've traveled the length of the Ohio River quite a few times, writing articles and video documentaries about river history and culture. On some trips, I went by steamboat, but mostly I hitched rides on towboats, my favorite way to travel the waterways. And I can tell you this: Captain Coomer gets the river right. The sounds, the smells, the sights, the movement of the boats, the way the people talk. Reading these sketches, you can feel the warm steel of the towboat's deck rumbling under your feet.

You don't need to have traveled the river to enjoy these stories; I read most of them long before I began my own river adventures. When I started reading, I asked myself if I really cared about the horsepower of an engine or the length of a tow and ended up fascinated by such details, but only because I was laughing so hard at some of the anecdotes Captain Coomer tells. As he says, the river produces "a unique breed of people."

As I read further, I found myself thinking, "Why, the man's a poet." The episode called "Who Could Ask for More?" is a fine evocation of a glorious river day. Many of the others show a poetic appreciation and love of the Ohio. Captain Coomer experiences it in its many moods and seasons: calm and stormy, day and night, summer and winter.

Life on the Ohio tells much about the ongoing importance of the river and reminds the reader not to get too carried away by Mark Twain nostalgia. Many tend not only to associate the river with steamboat days but to paint those early days as leisurely and charming while, in fact, the steamboat in its glory was the fastest and most economical way of getting goods and people where they needed to go. And the captains hustled to beat the other fellow to markets, in some cases burning up fancy parlor furniture to make the boilers steam faster. The river's part in commerce and transportation has never diminished. The Ohio was the country's highway west in the early nineteenth century, and it remains a vital waterway today, moving some hundred and fifty million tons of cargo per year. Captain Coomer's stories show the working river as it is in modern times, with its immense towboats, gigantic lock and dam systems, and millions of tons of materials on the way to industries all over America.

The author writes of the diesel river from a unique point of view: that of the man in the pilothouse of working boats, actually moving barges of raw materials and steering the loads of grain, chemicals, coal, and other products that bring energy and industry to the Ohio Valley and beyond. From this vantage point, he lets the reader feel life lived on the busy harbor tugs and the towboats seen moving constantly up and down the Ohio, pushing strings of barges longer than three football fields. He tells of the frightening moments and difficulties of piloting and also of the "family" formed by the crew, who are out on the river for thirty days at a stretch with no stops. His work comes from long and authentic experience of the river. The son and grandson of riverboat men, he grew up on the river and never left. When not at the helm of a long-distance towboat, he piloted the busy, important tugboats (really miniature towboats) and managed a Cincinnati harbor. He has built boats—his own tug as well as an authentic old-time flatboat—taught river work at Cincinnati's Inland Waterways Vocational School and, occasionally, for recreation, taken long trips down the Ohio and Mississippi.

Life on the Ohio adds a new and important voice to our river literature. It should find its place beside the many descendants of Mark Twain who have taken river stories into modern times: Richard Bissel, Captain Fred Way, Harlan Hubbard, and recently James Casto. Bissel, in *My Life on the Mississippi or Why I Am Not Mark Twain*, wrote of his long love affair with the Mississippi and his forays into the boat business; Captain Way, in *Pilotin' Comes Natural*, wrote of his lifetime passion for Ohio River steamboats. Harlan Hubbard, in *Shantyboat*, evoked the Ohio River as seen by an artist drifting down the Ohio and Mississippi in a home-built shanty. James Casto, in *Towboat on the Ohio*, describes his eight-day trip on a towboat, giving fascinating lore and information about the Ohio's character and importance, her towns and people. Captain Coomer rounds out the picture of river life given by our storytellers. He also complements the work of Ohio River poets such as James Wright, John Knoepfle, and Richard Hague, who remind us that the Ohio River provides not only water and sanitation for the people of some thirteen states but nourishment for the soul and myth of the Midwest.

Captain Coomer offers one man's story of his many years on the Ohio and her sister waterways. His voice is authentic and unique. Yet for lovers of the river and her literature, it has a familiar ring. A well-read man, mostly self-taught, his talk is a mix of bookish English and down-home riverese. He quotes Melville in one sentence and cusses or lapses into good ole boy diction in the next. Like many river writers from Mark Twain to Captain Way, or real-life river men such as Captain John Beatty, he combines a love of reading and the written word with an appreciation of the colorful and casual talk of the river people. His collection of sketches exhibits many features typical of time-honored American storytelling: the aware but down-to-earth narrator, a waggish, humorous tone, the celebration of basic values such as hard work, honesty, and human potential to learn and change.

Sometimes the writer is a bit of a curmudgeon, sometimes a softie, always observant, wry, concerned for his fellow man, convinced of the value of life. He's an old-fashioned fellow, and that's fine. The river is an old-fashioned place in some ways. In spite of the technological advances, the monumental dams, the modern navigational aids and other ways of controlling the unpredictable waters, the traditions of work, speech, and myth-making among the people find their roots in the beginnings of river travel. Certain types bob up over the decades: the crusty captain, the boy dreaming of the riverboat as an escape from quotidian life, the showboater and braggart, the quirky old-timer.

Captain Coomer's sketches were written over a period of time, about a career that spanned thirty years. In his book, he divides the pieces into his early apprenticeship as a harbor manager, his years on the line-haul towboats that go from Pittsburgh to Cairo, a time-out adventure in a small boat, and a year he spent working a self-built harbor tug. They take us from 1948, right after World War II, to 1980. Like most river writers, Captain Coomer looks back on his career with a touch of nostalgia. Twain declared that the trade of piloting had already been ruined in his day by the dredging of the channels and the posting of mile signs and lights. The "improvements" took all the fun out of river work. His descendants continue to lament the passing of old ways. Maybe this dream of a golden age comes about because the river, by its very character, must always change. Yet the Ohio flows on, as it did in Twain's day, as it does in Captain Coomer's and as it will in the days to come. We hope it always will, sustaining new generations of people, bringing with it good stories, giving our life and literature a flavor that keeps us from being landlocked, and lets us—if only in imagination—take trips away from ourselves and toward other people and places.

Dorothy Weil

Three Types of Barges

Open Hopper Barges

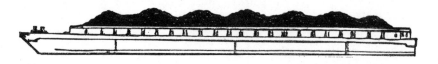

Type	Length (Feet)	Breadth (Feet)	Draft (Feet)	Capacity (Tons)
Jumbo	195	35	9	1,500
Super Jumbo	250-290	40-50		2,500-3,000

Covered Hopper Barges

Type	Length (Feet)	Breadth (Feet)	Draft (Feet)	Capacity (Tons)
Jumbo	195	35	9	1,500

Integrated Chemical and Petroleum Barges

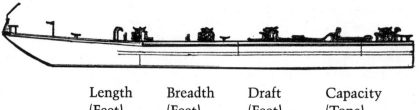

Length (Feet)	Breadth (Feet)	Draft (Feet)	Capacity (Tons)
150-300	50-54	9	1,900-3,000

Preface
The Ohio and Me

The river is a hard taskmaster. It has claimed the lives of some very good friends and has come close on several occasions to claiming my own. It has scared me out of my wits, raised my hopes, and dashed them in a moment. It has cost me my left thumb and a lot of my hearing. It has lost me money and a wife and has worked me to bleary-eyed exhaustion.

I made the decision to go on the river right after service in World War II, when I found myself faced with some dreary facts: I had no college education, in fact had not finished high school in my rush to join the navy. I was totally dissatisfied with my way of life. I had tried selling insurance, was a mess at it, and had moved on to driving a soft-drink truck. I had a wife, two and one-half children, and a staggering mortgage.

I am the son of a riverboat captain, who was the son of a riverboat captain, and I am the father of a riverboat captain. I guess I gravitated naturally to the water. So, to the dismay of my creditors and with a pat of encouragement from my wife, I decided that I had to go where I belonged.

I took a job as a deckhand on a harbor tug for a dollar an hour. Since then, I have spent my life working on the Ohio River and never have ventured far from its banks. Nor have I ever wanted to. In the ensuing years, I went from deckhand to port engineer, to pilot and captain on towboats pushing up to 24,000 tons of cargo. I've never made much money, but then I would never have made much at another line of work. I haven't the knack for it. Anyway, money makes me nervous and insecure.

I gained much more than dollars in my trade. When I was growing up, my father, a tough-as-nails steamboat captain and mate, had about convinced me that I couldn't pour piss out of a boot. On the river, I found confidence in my ability to do a good day's work, to withstand the elements, to keep my nerve in a tight place, and to do my share of the work alongside the toughest of my fellows. I awoke each day eager to get to my job.

Over the years I had experiences I wouldn't trade for a barge full of gold. And that's what this book is all about. The sketches tell of things I've seen and thought and felt while working on the river. They are jottings I made during some very lonely nights steering a towboat; they include recollections of some hairy moments and glimpses of people I could never forget.

Occasionally during my life I tried to cheat on the Ohio River and took time out to pursue other interests or tried working one of the other inland waterways, but I always came back to the Ohio. This river has been a persistent as well as hard master. Why do I love it so?

Maybe these sketches will tell you. I also hope they show that there is still plenty of interesting life on the old Ohio, that character and adventure didn't end with the steamboat. I am determined, too, to have the last word with the river that brought me so much and took so much away. This I say to my beloved adversary, the Ohio: "From the safety of the riverbank, I will tell all. I will write of my petty victories, that you may be sure will be vastly exaggerated. I will tell of our quarrels and of the great good times we had together. I will write of your good moods and bad. I will reveal your treacheries and make known your determination not to be taken for granted. I will warn all of your refusal to forgive those who are not wise and humble when within your grasp. And, finally, I will write about the unique breed of people who ply your waters and occupy your near shores."

I thank Rita Kohn, whom I met during her prodigious work on the Always a River project in 1991. The barge full of river exhibits fulfilled its goal of stimulating Ohio River projects—including this book—in towns from Pittsburgh to Cairo. The Ohio River Valley series of The University Press of Kentucky is a good example of continuing concern for our important and vital waterway, and Rita Kohn's suggestions and support have been helpful in bringing this work of mine to light.

Special thanks are due to Dorothy Weil, who labored mightily to help edit these sketches into a book. She got me to arrange the individual pieces in order and tie them together. She read and reread, criticized with sometimes brutal honesty, and cut with the dispassion and precision of a surgeon—occasionally going so close to the bone that it hurt, but saving some lives. Her scalpel sometimes had blood on it (mine; I mean, we had some real go-rounds!), but her faith in the work never wavered.

I am also grateful to the following people for their labor in going through their memorabilia, files, and scrapbooks to locate photographs: Chuck Parrish, historian, United States Corps of Engineers, Louisville, Kentucky; Ralph Plagge, former chief dispatcher, Ohio River Company; Bob Gray, former chief of maintenance, Ashland Oil and Refining Company; Captain C.W. Stoll; and Patricia Murphy Kuhr. Thanks also to Alice Loving, who created the artwork. Unless otherwise noted, all photos are from the author's collection.

Harbor Work
1948-1955

I Begin

When I was driving my soft-drink truck after the war, I was living with my wife and kids in a housing development. Enter one Jack Meade, who lived in an adjoining apartment. Jack was a handsome, dashing young man with a lovely wife and four beautiful children. He had flown solo at sixteen and was copilot on a souped-up DC-3 that was the executive aircraft of a large grocery chain.

When Jack went to work, he wore Ghurkha boots, a Hotshot Charlie 50-mission cap, and a genuine leather flying jacket. By God, how I envied him. I could very easily have disliked him for the same reasons I admired him, but he was such a nice person and wore his dash with such cool and lack of condescension that all I could do was try to be more like him.

I, too, had a lovely wife and beautiful children, but I had never been accused of handsomeness; dash I left to others and cast my lot with a lugubrious and stuffy dignity, which was a safe haven but not calculated to make me heroic in my own eyes or anyone else's. But most ignominious of all, I went to work in a silly uniform bearing the colors of that soft-drink company. It was not for me to burst the surly bonds of earth but rather only pop bottles. It was not for me to leap any continents: the old International truck and I never got farther than Madisonville, a small suburb of Cincinnati. My copilot dipped snuff, drank raisin jack, and liked large ladies.

The only thing that sustained me in those early pre-river years, as I endured the grumbling of loutish grocery clerks and the incessant urging of route supervisors for ever greater sales of their bottled poison, was the daydream of somehow escaping this mean little existence and joining the ranks of those who held command.

Oh, to be among men who braved the elements, who showed the finger to the beckoning Mr. Bones, who had dash and poise, who were secure in their mastery of great machines. Men who could swagger without the appearance of doing so, whose magnetism spoke of worlds not meant for ordinary people such as you and I.

That all this would someday be my lot, I doubted not. I grew up reading about King Arthur and the Knights of the Round Table, and Charlemagne and his Paladins. I had a whole pantheon of heroes: Rudyard Kipling, "Chinese" Gordon, Ulysses, Hector, Admiral Byrd, Jack

The *Pat Murphy*, a typical harbor tug of her day. Note the towing knees at the bow, where barges may be attached (courtesy of Patricia Murphy Kuhr).

London. One cannot possess a head full of heroics, good health, and a reasonably nimble wit and remain forever a purveyor of pop! And I did not.

When I heard that an old friend and owner of a nearby tugboat harbor was seriously ill and looking for help, I paid him a visit to see if he might need my services. My friend was a hook-nosed, tough, bandy-legged little Irishman who had been a hard-hat diver in the navy. His operation consisted of several harbor tugs, a retired barge known as a Valley Square, and a really worn-out old coal barge converted to offices, workshops, and a galley. It looked like home to me.

To my great surprise, my friend offered me a job as a deckhand on the tugs, with the stipulation that if I liked it and could do the job, in six months I would become manager of the whole operation. I jumped at the chance. The next day I was down at the Ohio River, checking out his largest tug, a 600-horsepower, sixty-five footer that he and several friends had built. She was a beautiful boat, well-designed, powerful, in short, the best in the harbor, which boasted two more of its own boats and six others belonging to competitors.

The tug was called the *Pat Murphy*. She was a little top-heavy, like all harbor tugs, which are basically small towboats. Painted white with green trim, flying the American flag, albeit a mite grimy, she was a fine sight. The towing knees at the bow, two structures that butt up against barges and look like a pair of giant knees, spoke of her function of re-

A typical long-distance towboat, bigger and more powerful (4,000 to 8,000 horsepower) than a harbor tug (400 to 600 horsepower) (courtesy of Ralph Plagge)

trieving barges from tows and fleets and doing other miscellaneous service jobs in the river industry.

I stepped aboard and looked her over: the small galley and supply rooms were in good shape; the pilothouse up top was well equipped with radar, depth finder, and all the other paraphernalia in use today. Then I entered the engine room.

As much as I loved the steamboats of my father's day, in the navy I had learned to love the smell of diesel oil. My ship, the USS *Biscayne*, was designed as an amphibious landing command ship; she was diesel-powered and slow, with eighteen knots as her flank speed. I was a motor machinist's mate or "MOMM." I spent my duty time in the forward engine room tending what I thought of then as two huge engines—though I have since seen diesels in cargo vessels that could almost fit one of the *Biscayne*'s engines into its crankcase. I loved everything about my work and was very sorry to leave the ship.

Since I had come home and begun working at those jobs I was so uninterested in, I had missed my diesels and the hot powerful odors of an engine room. When I smelled that diesel fuel and looked at the two big Cat (Caterpillar) engines of the *Pat Murphy*, I was hooked! I took the job of deckhand on her, for that big dollar per hour!

Hands On

The first time I stepped aboard the tugboat *Pat* as an official employee, I was so happy I couldn't wait to start to work. It was near sunset, a crisp, beautiful, early autumn evening. The Kentucky hills across the river from us were just beginning to show their colors, and the slightly brownish untroubled river flowed placidly, with only an occasional little whirlpool forming and quickly disappearing. The only sounds other than the peripheral hum of man at his twilight pursuits was the slap, slap, slap of small waves breaking under the sloping bow of the tug. It was great to be alive.

Or so I thought. I hadn't counted on the lead deckhand, a six-footer named Bushey who was much feared in the local bars, or the *Pat's* irascible captain, one Russell Lancaster, who made Queeg and Bligh seem benign. Nor had I realized just how backbreaking deck work can be.

The harbor tug is the workhorse of the river, a small version of the towboat that pushes enormous strings of barges to their destinations. The tug is used to deliver barges, crew members, groceries, newspapers, and mail to the bigger boats. The tug also pushes a fuel flat out to them, and fuels the towboats as they run dead slow in mid-river, for the towboats stop for nothing in their round-the-clock work.

On my first night aboard the *Pat*, we would be pushing barges from one location to another and delivering a wired-together set of eight barges to the *Valley Transporter*, one of the biggest towboats on the river. She was upbound now and would be approaching sometime during the night, expecting the addition to her tow to be ready. Her appearance at her estimated time of arrival would depend on how heavy traffic was at Lock 37.

Meanwhile, I had to get acquainted with our tug. Bushey was to serve as my mentor, but he didn't seem eager to share his knowledge of deck work. He was an unusual type on the river, a city boy, ferret smart, and a leader. His unnaturally flattened nose pointed to the pub brawls he was noted for. Like most river people, he was taciturn and somewhat suspicious of newcomers, who must prove their mettle to be accepted. He took me through my paces impatiently, never calling me by name. It would be a week before I was even "Coomer."

He began by introducing me to the engine room; there I looked over the two huge diesel engines, each about the size of a small car. It would be my job in the future to check the oil and the gearboxes and start the engines. They would be controlled as to speed and direction from the pilothouse. Our other, less modern tug required a deckhand to operate the engines under orders from the pilothouse. (When I became a pilot, I had some scary moments when those old-time babies would become air-locked. Once my engineer got drunk and fell asleep as we approached a lock, and no amount of yelling into the intercom seemed to wake him. We survived by my steering the boat into a muddy bank, running down to the engine room, and splashing a bucket of cold water on the man.)

After the engine room visit, Bushey showed me how to clean, fill, and trim the wicks of the kerosene fleet lights. These were warning lights that we would place on the thirty to forty barges we held in safekeeping for their owners in groups called fleets. When they were ready, we placed them on the barges, which are separated into fleets according to whether they are empty or full. After placing the lights, we took the *Pat* about a mile upriver, where we were to load rigging to assemble the eight barges for the *Valley Transporter.*

The trip was beautiful, the water black now except for intermittent reflections of the lights on shore. I perched on top of one of the tow knees and enjoyed the serenity of the night. I should have known better, but at the moment, I was completely content and eager to start work.

When the real work started, I was less happy. Not only was it hard and heavy, but I had no idea what was going on. In those years, even though I was young and strong, I weighed only 145 pounds, and every-thing I picked up or moved seemed to weigh more than I did.

We landed at the Mississippi Valley Line shop, an old steamboat converted into a machine shop, with blacksmith, paint, and engine-re-pair facilities. Staring at us were a great pile of chains, ten huge links to the section, and dozens of ratchets—devices for tightening the barge wires that held the tow together. There were dozens of coils of two-inch-thick line (rope) in lengths of sixty to eighty feet, and stacks of steel cable, an inch and a half in diameter and bristling with sharp broken strands that could tear into your flesh. Bushey and I must load all this "jewelry" (riverese for rigging) onto the *Pat* for use downriver. Fortunately, someone had told me to come to work equipped with heavy, leather-palm gloves.

When our chore was done, we headed back to our fleets. We must cull out the eight empty barges for the *Valley Transporter*. Now, a barge is a vast steel shell that can hold 1,500 tons of cargo. It is huge and clumsy, and picking one out of a fleet is about like picking a single cow out of a herd. Finding the ones we sought was particularly hard, because they were buried in the middle of the fleet, necessitating the moving of six or eight others. The barges were numbered, but not arranged in any particular order.

I was given the task of facing up or wiring the *Pat* to each barge with steel "face" wires placed over the barge timberheads, then cranked "fiddle-string" tight by means of hand-operated winches on our tug's main deck. Then came the really hard work of distributing the rigging from the *Pat* to the loosely assembled barges and wiring them up into a tow or a unit to be put into the bigger boat's tow. Bushey laid the wire cables in their proper places, with me carrying the ratchets, chains, lines, toothpicks, and cheater bars—the super-heavy steel equipment used in getting the barges wired together. All this slowed me down a mite, and I wondered if this ungodly labor would ever end.

We were in pitch dark, except for the carbon arc searchlights Captain Lancaster shone on the small space where we worked. If we turned toward the light, we were half-blinded, but beyond us all was black. We didn't want to misstep, for that might put us too close to the edge, or to the wires, or into the river.

Eventually, it was time to tighten every wire holding the barges into a unit. This was done with a ratchet, a seventy-pound cranking device the deckhand must work back and forth to pull the wires so taut you could jump on them with no spring back. Once assembled and wired, the barges were ready for delivery.

The *Valley Transporter* had arrived and was idling in the channel awaiting us. She was brand-new and one of the most modern and powerful towboats on the river. Painted brilliant white with bright blue trim and topped by two huge stacks, she exuded power. Her 180-foot length and a capacity of 6,000 horsepower would allow her to run the lower Mississippi with twenty-five or thirty barges. Here on the more demure

A towboat—similar to the *Valley Transporter*—with thirteen barges, a nearly full load (courtesy of Ralph Plagge)

Ohio, she was working toward the maximum of fifteen barges, the number we could fit into our locks without taking the tow apart. (Standard lock size on the Ohio is 110 feet wide by 1,200 feet long.)

We arrived alongside this behemoth. The top of the little old *Pat* barely reached her second deck. Suddenly the barges we had assembled swarmed with deckhands from the *Valley Transporter*. In thirty minutes, this crew wired the eight barges we had delivered onto the side of their tow. With a tremendous blast of the big boat's air horn, she departed up the river, and the *Pat* and her crew headed toward the next job.

"Well, Bushey, about time to eat," Captain Lancaster called from the pilothouse. No mention of me. But I tagged along to the *Pat*'s galley anyway. It was now my pleasure to meet that man in the pilothouse, Captain Russell Lancaster, who had been watching over and directing our operations all night. He was lean as a cowboy, square in face and jaw, about sixty years old—what I thought of then as old. By reputation, he had eyes like a tarsier for keen night vision, and a temper to match the feisty little animal's. He barely nodded to me and proceeded to brew himself a pot of the blackest, strongest-looking coffee I had ever seen; it looked to be made with water from the River Styx. We three silently ate the food we had brought for our one meal of the night. The captain washed his sandwich and cake down with a full pot of his evil brew. Then he and Bushey commenced discussing boat business, leaving me totally out of the conversation. They soon departed the galley, abandoning me to do the dishes and clean up. It was 2:00 A.M. by now, and I had made eight dollars gross. I felt as though I had lost the same number of pounds in body weight.

While washing the dishes, I could feel the boat moving, and when I finished, I went out to the front deck. We were on our way back to our fleet to pick up two loaded barges, one of bagged sugar and one of steel plate. We would deliver them to the Mississippi Valley Line terminal, about twenty-five feet from the shop where we had been before; there they would be unloaded by dockworkers. We were soon involved again in digging barges out from among others, this time from our loaded fleet instead of from the empties. Bushey remained a capable, but not encouraging or friendly, straw boss. No way would I complain or question any orders he gave; deck work is the basis of river transport, and I must learn it right before I could manage a harbor or run a boat.

At 3:00 A.M., we arrived at the terminal. The *Pat* had to move two other barges out of a very hard-to-get-to space in order to position our barges below a large stationary crane used for unloading. As new man, I got the job of making them fast: I removed the face wires holding the barges to our tug, thus freeing them from the *Pat*, while Bushey did the mooring—tying them off. Our next move was to shift the sugar barge to the terminal elevators, where it would be unloaded over the next two days.

By now it was 4:30 A.M. An hour to go until the change of watch and some respite for weary muscles. Orders for our next job read "Top [turn] MV 301 [a barge number]; spot [tie off] CT 4 at head of terminal for re-loading." This meant we had to find the specific barges with the designated numbers, which again might very well be wedged in and surrounded by several other of these monsters at the shop fleet, and place them beside the shop's work barges, so they would be handy for re-painting and repair in the morning. The work was repetitive, tedious, and tiring; we moved six or seven pieces of equipment and barges, then picked up two empty barges from the terminal shift and returned them to our own fleeting area.

At 5:30 A.M. we were finally finished, and we headed back to our harbor.

It was time to turn the *Pat* over to the day crew. Captain Lancaster descended from the pilothouse, preparatory to departing the boat. I had worked hard, done everything asked of me, and hadn't messed anything up too bad or let any barges go careening down the river. Bushey had furnished the brains of the activities and some of the brawn, but most of the heavy work had fallen to the green hand, me. I sort of wondered if the captain might give me a word of encouragement for a creditable first night on the job.

I said, "Night, Cap," in a cheerful, friendly way.

He just gave me a bored stare and demanded, "You didn't piss in the river, did you?"

I soon learned that one of the captain's obsessions was the disposal of urine in the river. He would fire a man he caught taking the quick way to relieve himself instead of using "the head." Russell was convinced that the couple of ounces of liquid waste a man could produce might somehow find their way into his next pot of coffee.

He would also fire any deckhand dumb enough to light a match in his pilothouse. Throughout most of his career, which was before river radar, pilots depended on knowledge of the river and excellent night vision to pilot safely after dark. He still did not make frequent use of radar, because of his training and because ours was often not working. Since men still often carried wooden matches, occasionally some green deckhand would wander into the pilothouse and fire up a cigarette with a big wooden torch, and ruin the captain's night vision just when he needed it most. They never did it twice. A crewman in his right mind would rather face an open boat and three thousand miles of sea than face Captain Lancaster in one of his Bligh-like fits of wrath.

Bushey headed up the hill as soon as the relief crew came aboard. I introduced myself to them. They also showed a minimum of interest in the new man. They were not in the least eager to hear the sea story of my maiden voyage, though I was about to bust a gut with the need to talk about my new experiences.

I plodded my way up the long hill from the harbor to the parking lot behind Joe's Bar where we left our cars. I thought over the night's work and found myself proud. I had done all right.

At 7:15 A.M. I arrived home a tired, contented man, kissed my wife and children, who were barely awake, got into the bathtub, and promptly fell asleep. Wife tucked me in at eight-thirty when the kids left for school. Tired, yes. Discouraged, no. I knew after one twelve-dollar night watch that I had finally found my calling.

Solo

I spent the six months after my maiden trip as a deckhand learning the many skills I needed to manage a harbor. I worked both day and night watches, and if I wasn't too tired after my watch, I would stay over a few hours and work with the welders and acetylene torch cutters and painters. I learned to service the big line-haul boats, make out the harbor's payroll and keep the books. I worked twelve- and fourteen-hour days and seldom got through the night without an emergency phone call. I loved it all.

In learning to run the harbor, I had the help of "Jumpin' Joe," the temporary harbor boss. Joe was a good fellow and treated me with friendliness. He kept the gas-powered barge pumps running, repaired electrical devices, serviced the barge crane, and supervised the barge cleaners and painters. I suspect he also submitted reports to the harbor owner as to my progress.

Piloting the tugs was one of the important, and more interesting, skills I needed. In those days, one man "learned" another the craft (the verb "to teach" is not used much on the river), so I needed a mentor to take me on. It took Captain Lancaster, the fearsome martinet I spent my first night on the river with, six weeks just to call me "Coomer." He was not about to take a neophyte under his wing, much less for the purpose of learning his job. I would have to find someone else to learn me piloting.

We had two other pilots. One was a real cowboy, and no one to emulate, though I occasionally rode with him. My real education came from one Bob Schletker, our senior captain and the best harbor pilot I ever knew. Bob could have piloted the bigger line-haul boats as well as our tugs, but he was married to a lovely, feisty, diminutive Italian woman named Rose. She loved Bob dearly and would not permit him to be gone for thirty days at a time. In fact, if I sent him on a two- or three-day trip, the phone would ring off the hook and I would come in for my share of Rose's ire. Because of Rose's devotion, Bob got the best-packed lunches of the whole work force. They always included Bob's favorites, a slice of chocolate cake and a big dill pickle. We all watched in great hilarity and with much teasing as Bob would take a bite of pickle and a bite of cake and chew them up together.

Except for his eating habits, Bob was my role model. With him and occasionally others in charge, I did considerable piloting. I acquired a degree of confidence and skill, but not enough to avoid a certain nervousness if they went below for a cup of coffee or a chat with the deckhand.

"Just keep 'er in the middle of the river, Jim, and you'll be all right," they'd say. I felt some reassurance that they were within shouting distance and only seconds away if I suddenly found myself looking at a bridge pier dead ahead, or worse, an oncoming towboat pushing fifteen barges.

I took my tests, not too arduous in those days, for an operator's license. These were administered at the Coast Guard station on River Road and consisted of written questions about the location of buoys, shore lights, and bridges, the meaning of warning lights, the rules of passing, and many other things important to know. Upon completing the test successfully, I was ready to pilot.

Well almost. There comes a time in a would-be pilot's life when he must do it all by himself. He is not always ready and may crash, crumble, and burn or sink a barge or boat. One cold January morning, though I didn't know it, my day of reckoning came. Had I known I would have stayed in bed.

On this fateful day, two of our boats had just finished taking barges out of the tow of an upbound long-haul towboat and were long gone delivering the barges to their assigned terminals. I was in the office doing the payroll, when after a long stretch of self-pitying muttering to itself, the radio squawked and sputtered into life. The call was from the long-haul boat, who was by now well upriver opposite Dayton Bar, about seven miles above our landing. The pilot informed me that his office had just given him orders to drop another barge at our fleet. Could we get a tug up to him and pick it up?

I thought that one over. The only boat we had available was the *Tim*, a small, ugly, underpowered harbor tug that the pilots hated. The only men left at the harbor were a skinny nervous night watchman with a bad stutter, who had never been on a tug boat in his life, and a neophyte pilot who had never soloed, namely me. I didn't dare say no. The owners of the towboat needing our services were our best customers. Rather than run up the hill and home, I mustered my courage, and in as confident a voice as I could squeak out, said, "Yessir, Cap, I'll be up there and get that li'l feller just as soon as possible. 'Bout an hour I'd guess."

"Got that okay, Cap," he replied, "I'm all stopped and jest holdin' these here barges in the middle of the river." He cleared the channel, as did I. Another voice came over the radio and said, "Good Luck, Captain," and I could swear I heard snickering in the background. "Smart asses," I thought.

My night watchman and I got untied without losing him. I came ahead on both engines and nothing happened but a dead silence and a slow drifting backward downriver. My "deckhand" and I had forgotten a rather important step in boat handling, and that was to check the oil and start the engines. I tore down to the engine room and kept a nervous eye on the fleet of barges directly behind us. Thank God, the engine fired up without so much as a groan, and I was back in the pilothouse in seconds, and once again came ahead on the engines. The fleet was only about twenty feet behind us, too close for comfort, when the two forty-five-inch props took us out of danger.

As we got under way, I remembered everything I'd learned and had the boat under control. I forgot all about my recent stupidity. "Piece of cake," I thought.

When we arrived at the towboat stopped in the middle of the river, I found to my delight that the loaded tank barge was in the clear on the outside of the tow. This meant no taking the tow apart to get at the barge. We just faced up to the square end and, with the help of a towboat crewman, got the face wires on. My watchman/deckhand could never have done it alone. He was a good night watchman, but decking was not his job, and his sinews were not designed for this work.

The barge crew turned her loose and the big boat and remaining tow eased on up the river. I waited until she was all clear of our barge before starting to "top" (turn) around and head back to the harbor. I maneuvered so as to place the side of the hundred ninety-foot barge into the current, a strategy that aided the turning process. Steering that length in a conventional manner would result in running out of river width and ending up on the far bank. Good thinking, Jim, I said to myself.

We approached the first bridge of the six that then spanned the river between Cincinnati and northern Kentucky. The next few miles were a bad place to meet upbound traffic, especially for a pilot on his solo trip. I called on the radio for any upbound boats heading our way. There was no answer, so we had clear river all the way to the harbor. Lucked out again!

I came full ahead on both engines. We were booming down the river at a hair-raising ten miles per hour, there was plenty of river room for one barge, and I was feeling mighty good about the whole operation.

I reared back in the pilot's chair, my feet up on the console, just like

A towboat negotiating one of the bridges in Cincinnati's tricky lineup (courtesy of Ralph Plagge)

I knew what I was doing. A cup of coffee would have been right welcome. I was truly enjoying myself, feeling confident and professional. I knew then that piloting harbor tugs, and some day, big line-haul towboats was all I ever wanted to do.

Unfortunately I forgot that we were heading downstream in a fairly good current, faced down on a square-ended barge drawing nine foot of water and loaded with fifteen hundred tons of cargo. I forgot I would have to get this thing stopped, turned around, and placed in our fleet. The deep draft and square-end design of the barge, along with the low horsepower of the boat, meant that backing her to a stop was next to impossible. But I was euphoric, dumb, and happy, and we went sailing right past the harbor still full ahead. My first solo was about to come a cropper. When I woke out of big-time pilot daydreams, we were a half-mile below the harbor and still coming full ahead, well on our way to Louisville.

I put the engines in full reverse, and except for the engines almost jumping out of their beds, nothing happened. There wasn't a hint of slowing. We were by then a mile below the harbor. Even if we could get our load turned around, we would be a long time shoving it back upstream to the fleets.

The little tug was not able to stop the barge by my backing on the engines. I tried to steer the barge around upstream and home. We got halfway into the current, which was now pushing us downstream broadside, and the nine-foot draft and length of the barge increased our problem. To continue pushing ahead just had us crossing the river and heading for a yacht club on the Ohio shore. The little boat just didn't have enough "ass" to get the bow upstream.

I could see, looking upriver, that one of our tugs was back home. My hand started to reach for the radio and ask for a little help. But I'd be damned if on my first solo trip I was going to holler uncle. There was no great danger, except to my pride.

Then something occurred to me that I had seen done, and that was to use good old terra firma for brakes. I steered the head of the barge back downstream and into the muddy Kentucky shore. We created a miniature backwater in the bank, which became known as "Coomer Holler," and no doubt moved the state of Kentucky a few degrees south.

This maneuver stopped the barge right sudden, and the boat and the back half of the barge started to swing downstream and we were able to get pointed in the right direction and back to the harbor. We were an hour and a half late.

I took my licks from the other pilots and harbor crews about my unfortunate first time at the sticks. Of course, I claimed I had planned everything exactly the way it turned out

Roots

I had some real experiences during my first river job, many hair-raising and a lot funny. But before I continue the stories of my early days, I should tell something of my background and how a soft-drink truck driver and miserably failed insurance agent became a riverman.

Both my grandfather and father were steamboat captains, getting their respective starts on what were then the headwaters of the Cumberland River in a tiny backwater called Burnside, Kentucky, now

90 percent under Lake Cumberland. My father made a half-lifetime career of it. My grandfather was not so lucky. In the winter and spring months when the river was deep enough to navigate, Grandpappy was a boat captain. In the summer, when it was too shallow to drown in, he was the town marshal of Burnside. Unfortunately he was a mite overzealous in his duties and got killed by a bootlegger. The celluloid collar he was wearing on his demise became a family heirloom with its neat little bullet hole plumb-square in the back. This does not mean that he was withdrawing posthaste to previously prepared defenses and could thereby be seen by some to be running away. It was rather a classic "Code of the Hills" situation, where the rules held that from behind a tree and in the dark of the moon was a perfectly honorable way to dispatch a marshal or any other man with the temerity or bad luck to find your still or "Blind Tiger" (back country for "point of purchase").

Fortunately for my father, town marshal jobs were not hereditary. He began his river career at the age of eight years as a boy-of-all-jobs on a steamer named the *Joe Horton Fall*, a regular visitor to Burnside. As he grew older, bigger, meaner, and tougher, he matriculated to the job of second mate on bigger boats and bigger rivers like the Ohio, Mississippi, and Missouri. As I recall him, he was the hardest, quickest-tempered man I ever knew. He too got shot in the line of duty. By a drunken roustabout. The bullet he caught went into the calf of his left leg; fortunately for him and ultimately for my sister and me, it was not fatal. After beating the roustabout with a capstan bar, he limped off to patch his leg and change his sock. What became of that sock, no one knows, but it for sure didn't become a family relic destined to join the hallowed collar of his less fortunate daddy.

Surviving his bullet and a later knife attack as well, my father continued on the river. He served on some thirty steamboats throughout the 1920s, usually as mate. The boats were packets, those single vessels that carried freight as well as passengers, stopping at every little landing and hamlet, and entering the country's lore for their glamour and the colorful characters that ran and rode on them. Late in the decade, decked out in gold-braided finery, as first mate on the second *Island Queen*, he met a lovely little four-foot-eleven flapper named Mildred Beamer. They were instantly and mutually smitten and, unlike his deep-water brethren who boast a girl in every port (though I doubt not that he had such, for he was a brave, cocky, and very handsome man), he got married.

My earliest home was a steamboat, the *Valley Queen* of Omaha, Ne-

The *Jo Horton Fall*, loaded to the "gunnels." The first deck of a packet was for cargo, the second or "boiler" deck for passengers, the top or "Texas" deck for sightseeing, plus officers' quarters and the pilothouse atop.

braska. Once a packet, by the time I lived on her, she was an excursion boat in the summertime and a frozen-in hell in the winter. In summer she was a place of creamy whips, dancing, and romancing, and to those who could afford it in this the beginning of the Great Depression, a palace of excitement and pleasure. My father was captain on her.

We lived in a tiny cabin, warmed in winter only by a pot-bellied stove. I helped my father carry water and coal for cooking and bathing, and helped break up ice around the hulls of the boat and john boats. One of my earliest memories is of getting stranded on a big piece of thawing ice: the small boat encased in it and I went sailing down the river. I was surprised, then scared and lonely, as I was pulled by the white, swift, icy current. I started yelling and waving. The Coast Guard finally caught me and returned me to the *Queen*.

Our life on the *Queen* came to an end when she hit a sandbar and sank. Fortunately, it was very shallow water, and the passengers waded

The *Valley Queen* (the *Jo Horton Fall* converted into an excursion boat) was our winter home when I was a preschooler. During the excursion season we moved to a hotel in Omaha, Nebraska.

ashore with no loss of life. Pappy as Captain was the last man to leave her. No one got wet much above the waist. But the newspapers made much of it and of him, being as they were a little short of news out there on the Great Plains. He became a hero, the last man to leave the stricken vessel in the great tradition. In the family archives there is a yellowed front page with pictures, eyewitness accounts, personal vignettes and a huge picture of Captain Pappy in full regalia shouting instructions to the departing passengers through a megaphone. When all were safe, if a bit damp, my father descended to the main deck and saved himself. I wasn't aboard during this melodramatic demise of a once noble vessel, but to my young eyes and imagination, it was all very exciting and heroic. We all looked on Pappy as a genuine hero, and he was, for even if this had been a major catastrophe, he would still have been the last man off. He was that way.

There was a seemingly endless supply of bitter winters, though the sinking of the *Valley Queen* came when I was just starting school. At that time the Depression had virtually brought the country to a stand-

Family scenes on the
Valley Queen (Mildred
Coomer)

still, and there were no more river jobs. Our family wandered about the
country like Okies, and my proud, once gold-braided father, master of
great vessels, was reduced to selling patent medicines in five- and ten-
cent stores. He sold sponges, made scrapbooks, worked in sleazy restaurants, and held myriad other less-than-heroic jobs. But he never stood
in a bread line, and his family never missed a meal—though there were
some prepared by him that my sister and I fervently wished we had
missed. I am sure that we will never forget his spaghetti with sardine
sauce, a foul concoction that we children gagged on, but which he ate as
though he enjoyed it.

Despite the Depression and the unappetizing foods, the thirties were
exciting and interesting. We lived in many different cities and states. Our
father never gave up searching for work, and our mother, the sweetest
person in our world, was the glue that held us all together.

But all things pass, and eventually Pappy got work again on steam-

The wreck of the *Valley Queen,* which hit a sandbar May 17, 1936, at Omaha. The pilot was at the helm; my father, who was captain at the time, was not held to be at fault, and there were no casualties.

boats. They were towboats this time, not excursion vessels, and there was no gold braid, only coal dust.

Finally we Okied our way to Cincinnati and never moved from the environs of this city, where there operated a huge, glamorous excursion steamboat, the second *Island Queen.* My father hired on as First Mate and once again wore the treasured gold-braid-laden uniform, exceeded in splendor only by that of the captain.

Mother, little sister, and I rode the boat almost daily until the feminine two-thirds of the trio tired of it. The male third, me, could not have been beaten off with a capstan bar. I was a natural born river rat and never wearied of the trips to Coney Island, a spectacular amusement park, and back to the Public Landing. As unpaid assistant to the First Mate, I got to help clean up the pilothouse and do other lowly chores. I was allowed to call the deck crew by name, and the Olympians (the officers) by their rank and last name. These latter gentlemen were the Captain, the Pilots, the Purser, who was in charge of all things financial, and the Chief Engineer—who was to bring about the boat's demise in 1947.

The two pilots, the famous Dosses, Captain Harry and his son Captain Wesley, were aloof in manner, cadaverous-looking, and utterly competent at their trade. They were a power unto themselves. Even the

"Captain Pappy" in full regalia on the Texas deck of the *Belle of Louisville*—not a man to be sassed, as indicated by his razor and knife scars from packet boat days. He died at age eighty-seven, and as a World War I veteran was buried in a military cemetery in Burnside, Kentucky.

Captain exercised no real authority over them unless they were dead, dead drunk, berserk, or were operating the boat in an unsafe manner.

Aside from their acknowledged piloting skills, the Dosses could fill a spittoon faster than I could empty and sluice it out—a job that fell to lucky me. But a small price to pay for being permitted to occupy the sacrosanct confines of the pilothouse, a place strictly off-limits to everyone on the boat, excepting only the Captain and First Mate and me. The boat's officers were such masters, and garnered such respect, and had such interesting lives, I believe it was because of them that I began to feel the first stirrings of my own ambitions to be a riverman.

After a couple of years, my father left the *Island Queen*, and we moved on up the river to Cincinnati's East End. There Pappy took a job as harbor master of the Cincinnati Yacht Club. Again the onerous chores of living right on the water fell to me. As on the old *Valley Queen* in frigid Omaha, my lot entailed carrying numerous buckets of water from the spigot on a hill above the harbor, up three decks to the little two-room cabin we occupied on the top deck. Toting buckets of coal and armfuls of kindling were my responsibility, and of course the always-mid-night-or-three-A.M. emergencies that required sparring the floats that had been pulled away from the bank by the current or winds. Breaking ice from around the headboat and keeping shore lines always tight were also jobs I helped my father do.

In the summer, I was a real Huckleberry Finn. My sister was right behind, trying everything I did. We swam the river and dived from the third deck of the club boat. We explored the banks in mud up to our thighs—cool, gooey, wonderful mud. We wanted only one thing of life: to find a dead body in the river like the ones we read about in the pa-per—or at least a chest full of treasure. During flood time, when we had to take a rowboat to get to school, we did find a trunk, but when we finally, in great suspense and anticipation, got it pried open, all we found was a solitary black bug. Still, discovering the trunk, like finding a pig washed away from his happy sty by the floodwaters, became, with time, a magic moment.

Watching the river from our snug little cabin, I began to have some serious ambitions to be a river man. Seeing the *Island Queen* and the numerous steam-powered paddlewheel towboats like the *Orco*, the *Omar*, the *Herbert E. Jones*, and the gigantic *Sprague* going by pushing huge tows of coal barges suggested that there was a life to be had on the river beyond wet-nursing fragile, cantankerous, permanently-moored yacht clubs.

I can date these days because I remember the family sitting at Sun-day dinner when the radio announced the bombing of Pearl Harbor. It seems that almost right away, our river days came to an end. My par-ents left the yacht club and went into the restaurant business. My sis-ter went to high school, and I spent a lot of time skipping school and staring out the window, dreaming of being a war hero. I lied about my age and joined the navy at sixteen but never became a hero. I did get to most of the countries of the Pacific Rim and rode out the infamous ty-phoon of October 1945. My time in the service added to my love of boats.

During those postwar years trying to go into landlubber trades, I was just kidding myself. But the Ohio River is patient, and just waited until I was ready to claim my place on her waters.

The Wrong Stuff

After six months of long hours and hard work, I was appointed general manager of the harbor. By then I was a proficient welder, boat and crew dispatcher, and office manager; my unfortunate start notwithstanding, I was a good pilot. I still had plenty to learn, but all in all I was feeling pretty confident. Surely, no one would blame me for wanting to show off a little to my neighbor and hero Jack Meade, he of the Ghurkha boots and the flying machines.

I called Jack one beautiful evening when business was slow and invited him and his wife to go on a ride with me and my wife on the tugboat *Pat*. We had a barge to deliver to the Valley Line Terminal. We would accomplish this small task, which would showcase my new mastery of boats, then have supper in the pilothouse, out on the river.

The wives, looking lovely in their summery dresses, brought on board a good-smelling basket of fried chicken and potato salad. I seated my guests on the "lazy bench" (to use a steamboat term—today, this is a three- or four-man plastic couch behind the pilot's chair, though the bullshit and griping that take place on it are probably about the same as they were in Mark Twain's day). Jack looked over the pilothouse with interest. "Shoot, Jim," he said, "this looks as complicated as our old DC 3."

"Well, Jack," I said, pointing out the various parts of the equipment, "these are the throttles and shifting controls, and those four rods are the steering levers that control the rudders, all hydraulically operated. This is the swing meter, this is the radar (as usual, it was out of commission). This is the intercom speaker, these are searchlight controls, and this is the two-way radio for talk between boats and shore facilities. Our call sign is WG 5123."

My old hero seemed suitably impressed, and I stood at the controls in the dusk, looking as commanding as a short, nervous man can.

I knew Jack was just being generous in comparing our work station and his for complexity. But at least this pilothouse was more impressive than my old International soda-pop truck, and I felt confident that my deckhand and I would bring credit on ourselves and our metier. Chance doesn't often come to a man to show his mettle in the presence of a hero, and when it does, the gods should see to it that things don't go awry.

My deckhand was a fellow named Jerry Baker, whom we sometimes referred to as "Little Bull" because he was built like a five-foot-tall circus strongman. He was a good friend and normally a competent worker.

I prepared to shove off. I hollered down to Jerry, who was on the deck holding the lines securing the boat. "Okay, pard, turn 'er loose!"

"Gotcha okay, Cap," he responded. "Will do." I loved him for that "Cap." Then he said, "Uh—you reckon I oughta fire up the engines first?" I hated him for that. "Ha, ha," said I, "sure thing," as though I knew all along they were not running. I'm sure Jack thought, "Who does he think he's kidding?"

A great banshee wail came from compressed air going into a starter motor, a great puff of bluish white smoke arose from one stack, and the boat came to life. Pretty impressive, I thought—that'll make up for forgetting to start the engines. Then the wail came again but no smoke, and then again and again, and then the sound of the nearly exhausted starting air fizzling out to a sigh. Jerry's voice came over the intercom: "Jim, I forgot to close the compression release. We gotta wait for the air to build up again." Well, I thought, maybe things will improve.

We finally got under way and headed for the fleet to pick up our barge. Jerry got the boat faced up without falling into the river or committing any other unprofessional acts, then turned the barge loose. By now it was dark. We started up the river toward the terminal, and as we did, I glanced back at the fleet. Well, lo and behold, there was another barge sneaking down the river all by itself. Good old Jerry, in turning our barge loose, managed to release the next one over as well.

"Well, well, " I said. "It appears we got another barge down there heading for Louisville all on its own." I tried to make it sound like we planned it that way, but of course, Jack knew better. Still he didn't say much, just sat there eating chicken and being pleasant.

We got the barge rounded up and tied off, then once again headed for the terminal about two miles away. This time we made it, even though I later wished we hadn't. I figured I had suffered enough mortification for one night.

The barge we were delivering was the type known as a Valley Square. It was 150 feet long, 35 feet wide, and had a huge deckhouse that made it impossible to see the whole front half. The cargo was bagged sugar, and the spotting had to be precise, the side door lined up with the terminal elevator. With these barges the deckhand has to stand on top of the deckhouse, give signals, and then scamper down the ladder and make the ties.

We approached the terminal wall dead slow. Jerry signaled, "Steady as she goes, all stop the engines and let her coast." I did. He started down the ladder, and the barge plowed into the terminal darn near head-on. The pilothouse was suddenly filled with flying fried chicken and bodies. I couldn't bear to look around. I didn't say anything, just gritted my teeth and wished I was somewhere else. Jerry popped back into view and decided that now that we had hit, to signal, "Head out."

"Jerry," I hollered, "why didn't you work the head out before?"

"Sorry about that, Cap," he replied. "I forgot my flashlight and couldn't see too well." I promised myself the pleasure of killing him slowly when the night was over.

Now we were parallel to the dock and sliding along nice and easy. Jerry signaled, "Kill it out," which means stop right there. I did. He disappeared. He reappeared. "Work it ahead slow." I did. He disappeared. He reappeared. "Back 'er down a lick." I did. He disappeared. He popped back up. "Head out, ahead slow." This went on for an hour. Forward, back, head in, head out. Jerry must have made forty trips up and down that ladder. A line broke. We knocked a chunk out of the wood buffer timbers. I was in such a state I couldn't even push and pull the right levers. And good ole Jack. Why, he just sat back there behind me chatting with the ladies and doing his best to ignore the whole farce.

By the time we finally got the barge spotted and were headed back down the river, I was wishing that I had stayed with my old soft-drink route.

Ever Get That
Run-Down Feeling?

Friends have often asked me, "Have you ever been badly scared in the years you spent on the river?" When I was a younger man, I would reply, "No, of course not." That was a lie. In the best tradition of the river it is considered good form to make light of even deadly peril, let alone minor frights. A genuine riverman who finds himself on a sinking boat and up to his waist in water and is forced to ask for help from another boat will say over the radio in a slow and deliberate manner, "Cap, I don't want to put you to any trouble, but we got a leetle problem over here. Do you reckon when you get done there you could sorta head over this way and take nine of us off this here boat?"

Now that I am older and have discovered that I am, after all, mortal, there is no reason to keep up the pretense of invulnerability. I have been scared dozens of times. I have been mortally afraid only a few times, but those are the times you discover what manner of man you are. Nobody but me will ever know how I acted in real danger; those were private confrontations. You will just have to believe that the bony old gentleman had his hands full and finally gave up on me to pursue less determined game.

He almost got me when I was piloting the *Tim M.*, an older and less lovable tug than the *Pat*. We had just placed an empty coal barge in a notch on the head of an upbound tow. The task required that we make a downstream landing, a routine harbor tug operation, and the two boats were facing each other with 1,000 feet of barges in between. The lines of the delivered barge were made fast, and my deckhand was up on the barge removing the face wires. When the boat was free, I told him I would pick him up on the side of the tow, and our job would be done.

I backed the tugboat away, turned broadside to the head of the tow, and proceeded to get out of the way. But just as the *Tim* was broadside, the pilot of the big boat decided to come full ahead on both engines. The bows of the lead barges hit the tug on the port side, pinned my pilothouse door shut, and rolled the little boat so far over on her side that the port propeller was almost out of the water. I found myself on the starboard wall, which had suddenly become the floor, with my hand braced on the ceiling, which had now become the wall. My foot broke through the glass window and my leg was in the river up to my knee.

This was one of those private confrontations with death that tell you a lot about yourself. Did I scream and cry and swear to be a good and God-fearing man if given another chance? Did I scurry around the trap like a frenzied rat and beat my fists upon the walls? Well, what I did was my business, and you will just have to believe that, since I am still here, I did none of those things but rather spent what could have been the last moments of my life before the tug rolled over and sank in beating off the hands of him who beckoned and coolly appraising what to do next.

What I did after those private moments was to pull my leg out of the window and slide down the wall, which was now floor, until I could reach the engine controls and radio. I jammed both throttles as far forward as they could go—which in the case of the port propeller was pointless since it was only fanning air—and at the same time I yelled over the radio, "All stop, Cap, God damn it, all stop." By this time, my boat was slanting over so badly that I started to slide back up the wall toward the ceiling, which was about to become the floor.

Well, I still don't know whether the other pilot got the message and did in fact "all stop," but that little boat of mine trembled and lurched forward on the power of one engine, while lying on her side. She stopped, then started once again as though she wanted to live as much as I did. There was the constant sound of breaking glass, which fell on me, and of rending steel as the handrail was torn off, the side of the pilothouse stove in, and all the port windows broken out.

Finally, with a mighty thrust, the *Tim* broke free of the head of the tow and popped upright like a cork, and I literally fell off the wall and onto the good old floor. Naturally, once both propellers got a bite at full throttle, she took off like a rabbit and, with the rudders hard down, did a quick suicidal circle and headed back for the front of the tow. It was only just in time that I got myself picked up and the boat under control before she put us right back where we had started.

Now was the time for reaction. I should have been blubbering with joy and nervous relief, but that would have been unseemly. So, overruling an instinct to head for the bank and up the hill never to be seen on the river again, I calmly circled around, picked up the deckhand, who said, "You oughta be dead," and started toward the landing.

The pilot of the big tow called on the radio and asked, "What happened out there, Cap?"

"Oh, nothing much," I replied. "You just sorta ran over me, that's all."

"You all right?"

"Sure," I replied, as though this happened all the time. "No problem, pardner."

His company would later receive a repair bill that couldn't reflect the damage done to me that day.

A Sticky Affair

Normally, unloading barges was not something we did at the harbor, but a sweet-talking fellow by the name of Roland Lindsey showed up one day with a barge full of molasses and proposed that we unload it for him. There would be many more shipments to come.

Now, syrup can be a tricky product to deal with. Honey is even worse. But blackstrap molasses is the worst of all. Most people are never confronted with these products in larger quantities than a pint or a teaspoon, but multiplying the small problems encountered by about one million provides some idea of what troubles a bargeload of molasses can cause.

This blackstrap was on its way to farm co-ops in southern Ohio and Indiana, where it would be used as a stock feed supplement. Once the cows got a mouthful of molasses-sweetened grain, Roland claimed, they never again would eat it plain. Getting the molasses from the scow to the cow was the problem.

Roland's plan was that he would moor each barge full of blackstrap alongside our headboat; we would mount a huge pump in the barge, run eight-inch hoses across the top and on up the hill to a tank that he would build, into which the molasses would be discharged. A fleet of tractor trailers would take it to its destination. He sweetened the offer with much-needed dollars, and we agreed to do business.

It was summertime, and the pumping was easy. The river was in pool, well-behaved, and the viscosity of the product was such that we could pump a bargeful up the hill in a day or two. But, inevitably, fall came, then winter arrived, and with it all that cold weather means to a riverman: ice, high water, low water, diesels almost impossible to start, and swift currents. The blackstrap became so cold and stiff you could almost walk on it, and it required steaming for days before it was thin enough to be pumped. So Roland, the Molasses King, brought in a boiler that looked as though it had been stolen from the Smithsonian Institution's collection of antique machinery. He installed it atop the hill and ran a steam pipe down to the bank and across the barge, thereby adding two more umbilicals to our headboat.

On really cold days that old boiler didn't put out enough steam to heat a small apartment, so by the time the steam reached the barge, it had condensed to a lukewarm trickle of water. About the only thing that boiler was good for was to furnish warmth to the men laboring at the molasses works, but since it was always on the verge of blowing up, it wasn't too helpful in that regard either.

Eventually Roland acquired a good boiler, and we were then able to discharge a barge in eight to ten days, if we were lucky. But in winter and spring there are great fluctuations in the river level, which necessitated tucking the headboat in when the water rose, and pulling it off the ground and out when the river fell. Normally this would be no problem. But with 1,300 tons of molasses barge hanging on the outside of the headboat, and all those pipes and hoses going up the hill, it became well-nigh impossible to get the headboat aligned properly without breaking something, and that something was always Roland's steam lines or pump hoses. As careful as we were, it happened repeatedly, and poor Roland became a raving madman before the winter was over.

One March morning, with the barge pump pushing molasses up the hill at a steady clip and Roland and me sleeping soundly in our beds (I slept at the harbor when emergencies were imminent), my telephone rang. It was a near-hysterical night watchman screaming that the molasses hose had ruptured.

On arriving at the scene, I saw that indeed the eight-inch rubber hose running across our barge had broken. The night watchman would not go near it, and the raw end of hose was whipping back and forth, spraying great globs of molasses all over everything. There was molasses hanging in streamers from the crane, the living quarters, the office doors and windows; it was all over the walls of the headboat and the walkway to shore, and about two inches deep on the barge floor. In the cold air it had become stiff and tacky, and defied all efforts to walk across it. We donned rubber boots, but the stuff would practically pull them off our feet. Finally, we got the pump shut down; with a couple of death rattle clanks, it upchucked a few more blobs of blackstrap, the last one catching me full in the chest and knocking me over onto the barge floor and into the two inches of molasses hardening there.

I almost pulled the seat of my pants out trying to get up, and of course my hair, clothes, and glasses were dripping with the stuff. I never hated an innocent nontoxic material so much in my life. We were days cleaning up that mess, a job compounded by a typically excitable Roland Lindsey. The weather didn't help, and it was well into spring before the blackstrap finally dripped its last, and the battle was over.

Almost. An even more heartbreaking debacle took place when I let myself be talked into cleaning an empty molasses barge that we had just discharged so that it could be loaded with soybean oil. The barge had to be absolutely spotless, and before the new cargo was loaded it had to be inspected by a marine surveyor and certified clean. The money for the job sounded good and business was kind of slow, so I decided we would give it a try.

Normally, barges are cleaned by high-pressure, superhot water and detergents applied by machinery. Of course, we didn't have any of those things. What started out as hard work soon turned into a round-the-clock nightmare, exhausting the entire workforce of our organization, including the boat crews. I had calculated thirty-six hours to do the job and figured to make a few bucks if we met that timetable.

Five days later, and with the whole crew on the verge of mutiny, the barge was spotless. Proud of the job, though exhausted, and despite losing a small fortune on it, I called the surveyor. He looked her over and told us what a fine job we had done. There remained, he said, one test. That was to blow steam through the barge's steaming coils to check for leaks. So we hooked up the steam and opened the valves. Someone in the past had failed to drain the condensed water out of the coils, and they had frozen and split on the underside in a hundred places and filled up with molasses. When the steam hit those coils, it blew molasses all over the cargo compartments. Our spotless barge was a mess.

Three and a half days later, the barge finally passed inspection and joined a downbound tow. Besides working the employees past the point of exhaustion, we lost about $1,500 on the job. So the next time you spill a little honey or molasses on your tabletop, just moisten your fingertip, wipe it up, lick it off, and count yourself lucky. And steer clear of sweet-talking entrepreneurs.

Everett Riley,
Last of the Muskrateers

It was my day off. But instead of heading for an easy chair and a book, I was out in a small boat puttering around on the river. I took along my friend Gordon Baer, a photographer. The two of us were fascinated by the recent appearance of a little fleet of boats moored on the Kentucky bank, half a mile below the Little Miami River. These four odd crafts had created quite a stir among river people in the area.

We borrowed our boat from a local marina and approached the moorage with a certain amount of caution. Rugged individualists—and we were sure the commander of this wee flotilla would be such a person—view uninvited guests with well-armed alarm. We hailed the landing from a good way out in the river, and in a moment a small man emerged from his "houseboat." He was wiry, bewhiskered, and well-nigh toothless, probably about sixty years old. He must have weighed around 115 pounds soaking wet. With a friendly smile, he waved us over to his boat. I have met some mighty rugged and self-sufficient men during my years of fooling around on the river, but this lean, tough, and, as it turned out, articulate little gent named Everett Riley was the all-time champ.

The flagship of his fleet was his houseboat, which he had acquired for five dollars and a used radio. It was twelve feet long and six feet wide, flat-bottomed, square-ended, and made of wood. Most of the deck area was devoted to Mr. Riley's living quarters, a seven-by-seven, four-foot-high structure containing a bed, a stove for cooking, and his main heater—a five-gallon can converted to a woodburning stove. The "cabin" also contained an auxiliary heater, clothes, and shelves. It was covered by a plastic roof that "hardly never leaks except maybe when it rains and blows real hard at the same time." For power, Everett had a small, homemade AC generator that "could be used for lights and other comforts," but he spurned such luxuries; he used the generator to power his table saw and electric drill. His only other concession to modern convenience was a pair of propane gas tanks to fuel the lights, the cooking stove, and the auxiliary heater.

Mr. Riley's home was cozy, to say the least, and had one distinct advantage: the occupant never needed to leave his bed for a day's indoor activities. He and I fit in the house quite nicely, but for six feet and two hundred pounds of photographer to get in also was asking a lot of it; Gordon sat on the deck.

Mr. Riley told us he was born in Wellsburg, Kentucky, of an Irish father and an Indian mother and had been making it on his own in one kind of river job or another since he was thirteen. When he was not off adventuring on the river, his home port was Hazel Green, Kentucky. There he assembled his fleet and had a house, a "piece of propitty," and a seventy-year-old wife who didn't mind a bit about his "taking off for a spell."

He had been and still was a trapper and had been a commercial fisherman until the "big shots" and pollution made that enterprise unprofitable. He had been a merchant seaman on ore ships in the Great Lakes, a boat builder, and a crewman on river towboats back in the age of steam.

The number two boat in the Riley fleet was a conventional metal rowboat, made distinct from thousands of her sisters only by a Rube Goldbergian powerplant, an old cast-iron single-cylinder engine, a museum piece that couldn't possibly crank out more than three horsepower. This prime mover of the floating stock was started by an oversized flywheel that set into motion a series of belts and pulleys defying description. Considering the tasks she performed, this boat had to be efficient and well maintained.

Number three in the fleet was the "boat" that Everett used for setting and checking his muskrat traps; it was an amazingly maneuverable craft that consisted of two old automobile hoods welded together. She had store-bought oarlocks and a pair of handmade oars.

And last but not least was Everett's most recent acquisition: an old wooden lapstrake runabout minus engine and seats. It served as a storage boat, holding spare traps, tools, gas cans, and a supply of empty beer cans for trap floats. Everett "swapped a guy an old wore-out pistol with a busted firing pin" for it in Wellsburg.

Mr. Riley was a self-proclaimed mechanical genius and inventor. His storage boat was half-full of old engines people had given him just to see if he could make them run. "And I will, too," he said. "If they run once, they will run again."

After swearing Gordon and me to secrecy, Mr. Riley said, "Boys, I'm going to show you something that they ain't nobody has ever seen!" With that he pulled from his wallet a dog-eared sketch of a coal-mine safety system he had invented. "All I want to do, boys, is save lives," he said. I

Trapper Everett Riley and
his "prehistoric" cast-iron,
three-horsepower engine
(*Cincinnati Post*)

still cannot reveal all the workings of that invention, having been sworn
to secrecy, but it involved hydraulic trap doors and aluminum life-support pods.

"They's millions in it for you boys if you want to help me develop it."

For his muskrat operation, Mr. Riley had selected as his trapping
grounds an area under a railroad bridge across the Licking River between
Newport and Covington. He had a catch of sixty-five muskrats, and the
going rate was a $1.35 per pelt (paid by the Samuel Wells Co. of Cincinnati).

"It was good trappin' up there and quiet water, but the day after I
got started, I had to go back to Hazel Green to pick up my pension check.
While I was gone, somebody stole forty of my traps, so I moved up here.
And I'm fixin' to move again to the mouth of the Little Miami River.
The wind swells and boat wakes in this long reach is fit to tear me up. I
figger whoever took my traps ain't usin' 'em, because if they was, I'd
know about it."

Everett's muskrat traps were of his own design, utilizing scrap wood
and empty beer cans, and he was planning to get a patent on them. "I

take stuff that other people throw away and make money on it." We had to admit that his muskrat traps were ingenious affairs. The actual trap was a simple, spring-loaded, small-animal trap of steel and therefore highly nonbuoyant. Mr. Riley had to figure a way to keep the bait visible on the water's surface to the swimming muskrat, and the trap invisible just below the surface, so as to catch the animal when it tried to reach the bait.

Here's how he solved this problem: he built an inch-thick wooden raft, eighteen inches long and twelve inches wide. Across the center of the raft and several inches above its deck, he fastened an ear of corn. The trap itself was placed on the stern of the raft, which was weighted so that it rode just below the surface and the corn appeared to be floating free. The empty beer cans fastened at each corner prevented the raft from capsizing. The entire affair was moored to a stake driven into the river bottom.

Now Mr. Muskrat, being a good riverman, always makes an upstream approach. With Everett's device, not only would he find a delectable ear of corn but a convenient platform on which to enjoy it. Except that the platform had a trap on it.

"I usually have about 150 traps on hand," he said, "but I never set out more than fifty or sixty at a time. I ain't tryin' to get rich overnight, and besides, I don't care to work that hard."

Life was not all industry and inventions to Everett Riley. He planned to visit old friends in the East End while in Cincinnati. "I like to go honky-tonkying once in a while." He advised us boys to follow his example and "leave the river to do your drinkin' and stay away from it till you're done. City people go to the river to do theirs, and that's why they get drowned."

I often wonder if there are still people who can make do with so little and enjoy it. Mr. Riley promised to be back in Cincinnati for many years to come "if the river don't get me first," but I never saw him again. Years later I wondered what had become of him, so I called Hazel Green, Kentucky, and talked to the mayor. He informed me that Everett had died in bed with his rubber boots off in 1992 at the age of seventy-five.

Daddy Cool and the Kid

Commercial riverboats, both tows and tugs, are called "shallow draft" vessels. Draft means how deep into the water the hull extends. The shallow draft (average about six to eight feet) of riverboats helps them to clear shallow spots in the river; nevertheless, in *extremely* shallow water, they can become unwieldy and cantankerous. It is a characteristic of these boats to suck downward when they don't have enough water or to try to climb the banks when operated too near the shore, so they become sluggish about answering the helm—that is, reacting to steering. They can paste themselves to the bottom of the river, and this tendency further complicates barge fleet shifting work, which is always done near the shore.

Parts of the Monongahela are very shallow, and every turn of the boat's propellers churns up great clouds of sediment. The upper reaches of the Kanawha at Charleston, West Virginia, are like this also. There you must spot a barge as close as you can get to the landing, then get on the outside and shove it sideways. But the worst place for shallow water and nerve-wracking landings is a place called Ft. Hill at Mile 489 on the Ohio. This landing consists of a huge, anchored derrick boat, and the barges we placed there were loaded with sulfur, a dry yellow powder that irritates the eyes and nose—the classic brimstone of antiquity. There was a sandbar just outside the derrick and lying parallel to it. Access to the lagoon—like the depths between the derrick and the sandbar—was cut off by shallow water at the lower end and a flotilla of moored coal barges at the upper end. This situation made it impossible to perform a nice, safe, gentle landing. You simply could not sneak over the bar. I know; I tried all one afternoon my first trip there, with just one barge. Finally, an old feller came out to us in a johnboat and said, "Son, you trying to get that barge in here?"

"That was my intention, dad, but I don't believe it can be done."

"Why, shore it can, son. Want me to tell ye how?"

"I reckon," I answered, looking skeptical and uninterested and sucking a jaw tooth like some fool hillbilly. This was years ago, of course, and I was somewhat younger and more smart-alecky. Since then, I have learned that men don't lose their marbles when they lose their teeth or lack for brains from being from the mountains. (I'm part Appalachian myself, what with my daddy coming from Burnside.)

"Well, ye just take her over to that there far bank," the old guy said, indicating the opposite side of the river about half a mile away. "Then you see that little farmhouse there on the hillside?"

"Yep, I see it, oldtimer," I said, looking at everything but him and the farmhouse. It sure galls a young Hotshot Charlie who reads King Arthur to be drawled at by an old cracker.

"Okay, son, you just line your stern up on that farmhouse and your head on this here derrick boat and come full ahead on 'er and don't stop."

Well, I'll tell you, that sure got my attention in a hurry. I may have been a hotshot, but I wasn't crazy yet. In a half-mile I'd have 2,000 tons moving about ten miles per hour, and that is a force to be reckoned with. "Why, dad, you must be crazy or think that I am. I'll knock that derrick boat plumb into the next county."

"No, ye'll not, boy," he chuckled, "and ye'll not get in there if ye don't do it that way."

I guess that "boy" did it. "Okay, dad, I reckon if it can be done, I'm the feller to do 'er. Just keep you and that little boat outa my way."

"Don't worry none about me, son. I'll see ye at the derrick boat," he said and took off.

I took her over and lined her up and took off full speed. We were flat flying across the river, and I mean that derrick boat was getting bigger all the time till it damn near filled up the whole front window. My hands were sweaty and just itching to haul back on the throttles. You just didn't do things this way. Soon we reached the point of no return, where all the backing in the world wouldn't save that derrick boat or the foolish old man leaning nonchalantly against the boom, picking his teeth and grinning and staring sheer doom in its onrushing face. We were going to hit—I just knew we were—and I was about to throw myself on the floor and protect my eyes from flying glass and falling girders. The big old five-ton clam bucket was hanging out over the water just waiting to take its first bite of sulfur and grinning evilly because when we did hit I was likely to sail out the pilothouse window and right under it.

Just then there was a bit of a lurch: we had reached the bar, but small comfort—we'd take that out like a bulldozer. Then another lurch, stronger this time, and an almost imperceptible slowing took place. Another bump and scrape and we were slower still, though still coming full ahead.

Another bump and almost a stop, then a start, still full ahead. Finally, there was a long scraping groan from the load, and I could swear I saw that barge hump in the middle. Then we were over the bar and into the lagoon outside the derrick, and I put the rudders hard over starboard and cut the throttles. The head swung out just as pretty as you please. The ride over the bar had slowed us to near perfect approach speed, and she slid in alongside that derrick like a baby whale.

"Warn't nothin' to it, were they, sonny?" the old man called over to me, still tooth-picking cool.

"Sure wasn't, pardner," I answered, just as cool despite the alarm bells still clanging in every nerve ending in my body and the muted crackling as I acquired the first of the gray hairs in my beard.

That landing never got any better, and every time I had to go there and face the shallow water and Daddy Cool, who was always waiting and watching with supercilious concern, I'd have a quiet little nightmare about a gleeful Old Man River some night scouring away the bar and us sailing full bore into the derrick boat; the local heavens would be sulfurous yellow for days. But, you know, it would have been almost worth it to watch the sudden realization on that cool old face that this time we weren't slowing and to see him take his know-it-all ass up the hill just as fast as his scrawny old legs would carry him.

Biff! Bam! Pow!

There is an old saying that a good big man can lick a good little man anytime. At one time I doubted the accuracy of that statement and got myself into many a bar fight trying to prove it wrong. I was convinced that I, a small man, could be just as tough as my large, ex-river-captain father, who flattened everything in his path.

Fortunately for me, my river career did not begin until I had pretty well gotten over the youthful fancy that all big men must fall or flee before my fierce spirit. They seldom did, and I survived only because it was also my good fortune that some of my antagonists viewed my efforts to conquer with benign good humor. One such good ol' boy doubled me up and deposited me, with a good-natured chuckle, ass-first into a garbage can, then kicked it over. Upended and with only head, feet, and fingertips protruding, I must have looked like a badly designed turtle. By the time I had extricated myself from that unseemly repository for overmatched warriors, I had lost all lust for further battle. Besides, my bottom and back bore a considerable and damp collage of eggshells, coffee grounds, soggy bread, and old chicken bones. I wish I could remember what all this was about, but my youthful attempts at suicide were usually the result of bottled courage, and "reasons" didn't figure much into my battles. When the courage quotient soared, the efficiency quotient plummeted, and I frequently wound up hitting telephone poles, thin air, or the sidewalk, but rarely opponents.

That all this was behind me when I became a riverman was a very good thing. My delusions of being a David were gone. In the river business, however, sometimes you have to fight whether you want to or not. Once you start running, you might just as well keep right on running, up and over the hill to a safer occupation.

I faced a situation requiring fisticuffs with my old mentor Bushey one cold, foggy morning at about 6:00 A.M.—not a good time for pugilism. At that hour all systems are sluggish. Your spirit cries out for no greater challenge than pouring a hot cup of coffee. It is no time to be confronted by a huge deckhand determined to subtract from the total sum of your parts.

Of all the things I did not want to do that morning, the first was to fight what had to be a losing battle. The fierce spirit of yesteryear was nowhere to be found, and my courage level was about three quarts low. Even if my opponent had been Tom Thumb, I'd have had no stomach for fighting. In fact, Bushey was almost six feet tall and a solid 190 pounds; he was half drunk (thank heaven) and bent on vengeance because I had fired him the day before. By this time, Bushey and I had worked together for some eighteen months, during which his attitude, his sobriety, his punctuality, and my ability to count on him to show up for work had all gone downhill. I had plenty of reasons for my decision to let him go; however, this morning proved a verity: never fire a big deckhand unless it is the day before your vacation or you are three minutes from departing downbound with a fast tow of empty barges in a swift current.

On that fateful morning, I was by no means a ninety-pound weakling, but I was sure not in Bushey's class, and the outcome of our fight was inevitable. But my adrenalin was flowing, and he was some slowed down by a night of drinking and savoring the prospect of my demise. We went at it on the river bank where the *Pat* was moored. In about eight minutes, it was all over. I had picked myself up from the soggy bank four times, was winded, had the beginning of a black eye and a full-blown puffed lip and a bleeding nose. I was gratified to see that Bushey was breathing heavily and had a few superficial abrasions on the cheek and forehead. Somehow during the melee, I must have found a box to stand on to inflict those. Evidently satisfied that he had left me dead or dying, despite the fact that I was standing up, he got in his car and departed. I walked slowly, checking for missing or rearranged parts, down the hill to our landing. Once safely on the harbor barge, I had my coffee and recounted my adventure to the crew on duty. The consensus was that I got off lucky.

Within twenty-four hours the news was all over the river community that I had fought the legendary Bushey Foster and lived to tell the tale. My body hurt, but my pride didn't; even in losing, I had not lost my place in the river fraternity and had no reason to head up and over the hill.

Unfortunately, eternal verities seem not to stay with me very long. Soon after my wounds healed I again asserted my right to lessen the work force and fired not one but two men at the same time. They were young, and they were brothers; most important, they were dyed-in-the-wool, down-home country boys as thin-skinned as a third-degree burn where their honor was concerned. They considered bowie knives or bullets, not fists, as the only means of cleansing the sullied family escutcheon—and the degree to which it was considered sullied was in direct proportion to the amount of "moon" consumed before the ritual washing in the malefactor's blood.

"Jim," a quietly happy and expectant deckhand announced that day, "them S—— boys is a waitin' top of the hill for you and they're some likkered up."

A glance up the hill showed the two, both loaded and cocked, perched on a pair of concrete blocks. They each had a shotgun in an equal state of readiness. I considered abandoning ship and swimming to New Orleans but figured they'd be "settin' on the levee waitin'" for me when I got there. I had some time to figure out what to do, for they wouldn't dare to come on our "propitty." The code didn't permit that. But they damn sure could see that I didn't come "offen" it except feet first.

Now, my father would have walked up that hill and either gotten himself blown away or made sure there were two young country boys in a sad state of disrepair, each sporting the stock of a shotgun out of the seat of his pants. Well, I'm sorry, Daddy, but I'm some civilized, and though I don't mind gettin' my ass kicked once in awhile, I got no hankering for getting dead.

In my father's river days, the presence of a lethal weapon in the hands of an opponent was no excuse for being craven. You took it away from him or picked up a capstan bar and beat his brains out. But men were tougher in those days and didn't die as easily from bullet holes or knife wounds.

Some might ask why I didn't call the police. But in the river business, that would be a mistake. One thing rivermen and country men can't stand is an authority figure. The sight of a uniform, gun, or nightstick leaves no room for a man to play out his little "high noon" drama and save face. The uniformed officer—who can kill, if necessary, without regard for the code, without fear of reprisal, without preliminaries—embodies the vast authoritative weight of the citified society that formulates the rules that are anathema to the river- or country-bred man.

We counted on the probability that these young men were not truly homicidal but only affronted and drunk and that, given time and lack of money, would soon get sober and bored and go home with the satisfaction that they had kept that S.O.B. Coomer's head down and his hide hid in a steel tugboat for nigh onto five hours. I stayed busy at the harbor, and the boys finally sobered up or got bored and departed for home. Actually, they were both pretty good workers, and in due time I hired them both back, and with no problems.

Now I'm sorry, Daddy, if wherever you are you should read some implied insult here, but it is a fact that the more refined the brain, the more vulnerable the gut. Modern ballistics may have something to do with it, but we civilized folk who have not only heard of the ballet but have actually seen one kill easier than your generation. So I can emulate you only up to a point. A charge up what could have become a very sanguinary hill, I leave to you and presidential aspirants.

Moving On

Working at the harbor, I came to know the current sets (which way the current pushes) of every bridge pier; I knew every navigation light, every buoy, every landing, every acute bend in the river within fifty miles upstream and downstream of our operation. I learned to work with the other men, to operate a crane, to pump and repair barges—and God knows, after the molasses incident—to clean them thoroughly. After seven years doing harbor work I did not regret a moment of the time. I was, however, beginning to feel a vague discontent. As I worked around the Cincinnati area and serviced the huge long-distance towboats on their way to other places, I wondered what adventures and perils would beset them when their business with us was done. The constant local activity began to pale, and the greater upper and lower reaches of this beautiful river began to beckon.

One day, I stood on the bank and watched a fully loaded towboat sweep past. There was something majestic in the great white wheelwash rolling out from under the stern as the helmsman came full ahead on the boat's mighty engines, pushing the flotilla of fifteen barges before it. The cook and the engineer standing on the lower deck waved the two-armed river salute. Where were they going? What was it like getting to their destination? What was it like to be the pilot and to control all that mass and power, to know the river beyond our small bailiwick?

More and more, I felt I had to know. I must find out firsthand what it was like to be in that big pilothouse, feeling the slight vibration of maybe 4,000 horsepower beneath me, knowledgeable about all the arcane equipment that tugboats lacked. I was determined to join the elect who piloted those great vessels from Pittsburgh to Cairo and beyond. And it was clear that I would never get where I wanted to be by tugboating around Cincinnati.

I was well prepared for work on the larger boats. The harbor business is the best school for would-be long-distance pilots and captains; we had often handled six to eight barges with 400- to 600-horsepower tugboats. How much more difficult could fifteen barges be with 2,000 to 4,000 horsepower at your command? My job at the harbor became more of a drain every day; I grew tired of phone calls—most at two or three in the morning it seemed—from towboats passing through and

Here I am, looking forward to
a new phase of my river career.

needing some service, often menial. I grew less patient with pilots and
deckhands who didn't show up for work, leaving me to put in twelve-
and fifteen-hour days. My employer, who was back on his feet after his
heart attack, decided that returning to the river business would create
too much stress for his healing heart and bought a bar in downtown Cincinnati. He would be of little help at the harbor.

My wife and I had drifted apart. I had led her a hard and lonely life,
and we agreed to separate. (And we stayed that way for quite a few years.)
There was little reason not to try towboating. The thirty days on and
thirty days off routine would be a change, but maybe a good one.

I left the harbor and signed on as a pilot with a small river company
in Cincinnati. I would start out piloting a towboat named the
Ravenswood. She had belonged to Ashland Oil in her younger years and
had sailed under the name *Jim Martin*. Oddly enough, the man she was
named after was Jim Martin Lancaster, the son of my old skipper Russell
Lancaster, he of the pee phobia and the evil coffee. I had gotten pretty
friendly with Russell once he learned I was serious about the river; along
with Bob Schletker, he had given me many tips on piloting. I looked forward to my new life eagerly, maybe with a bit of trepidation.

The *Ravenswood* was a fine boat, about 145 feet long, 30 feet wide,

One of the glamorous long-haul boats I dreamed of commanding (courtesy of Ralph Plagge)

The towboat *Ravenswood.* She handled well, and I always loved her sleek lines (courtesy of Jerry Mueller and Wayne Supply).

and about 1,800 horsepower—by far the biggest boat I had ever steered. When I saw her at Southern Harbor, she was painted gray and looked a little drab. I decided she would look better with a fresh coat of paint, and soon after I started steering her, I put in for blue and white paint.

I loved that boat. She was one of many vessels I would serve on as pilot and captain, and the fine moments and adventures I remember from my new trade took place on a variety of towboats. But you never forget your first love and your first night alone together.

Towboating
1955-1980

A First Night

The first night I piloted the *Ravenswood* I could hardly wait to take over the levers. We would be pushing fifteen empty Ashland Oil tank barges to the company's fleet some 158 miles upriver. We were scheduled to leave at midnight. Though I was by then an accomplished pilot and had even taken as many as nine barges to Louisville and Portsmouth with the harbor tugs, I didn't know quite what this would be like. Despite my bravado, the small harbor boats don't compare with the big towboats, and the more usual two- or three-barge tows never seemed to stretch to infinity as fifteen barges can.

By the time we got to the fleeting area our barges were already made up into a tow—that is, they had been lashed together by steel cable into a unit. It was close to midnight, the time I was to go on the aft watch as pilot. I would be on duty until six A.M., then again from twelve noon until six in the evening. The captain stood the other two watches.

To me fell the job of facing up, or taking the boat up to the tow, where the two would be attached. I would stand by as the mate and crew laid two-way speaker cords for communication between me and the men on the head of the tow—the outermost barges, some thousand feet from the boat. They also ran light cords for the red and green lights marking port and starboard, and a middle amber light on the barges. These would warn other traffic of our presence and show where we were in the river, so that no pleasure boat would come roaring out of a yacht club and smack into us, and no others would think we were just part of the dark water. A jack staff was erected in the center of the tow and bore, besides the company flag, a very small white light that enabled the person steering to detect any swing in the tow and the degree of the swing. Of course, on foggy hazy nights we relied on radar.

At 12:45 A.M. the mate said over the speaker, "We're all ready, Cap, if you are. Nothin' but a headline left on her."

"Turn her loose and let's get out of here," I answered, with more confidence than I felt. That monstrous mess of barges out front stretched out forever into the darkness. We were at the lower end of the city of Cincinnati, at the Mill Creek outlet. There were faint bridge lights and even fainter shore lights on this stretch of the river, so visibility was not too good.

"All Gone!" the mate cried, which meant that the tow was free of restraints. I watched the crew on the barges amble back toward the boat, their progress illuminated by the flashlight each man carried, and my heart was full of love for them, for, neophyte that I was, they would do my bidding without more than a little grumbling.

A tow is a dangerous place even in daytime but can be deadly at night. As the men returned to the boat, they stayed in the middle of the tow and avoided the outer edges where a fall would land them in the river. Each flashlight was angled downward and slightly ahead of the man so that he could avoid the dozens of ratchets, chain links, and taut lengths of steel cables that held the barges rigidly together. Soon they were gone from sight and no doubt heading to the galley for a sandwich and coffee or a piece of cake. Food on a towboat is available twenty-four hours a day, and this one had a sweet, elderly widow in the galley, who could really cook.

The tow still lay against the side of the fleet but had started to drift slowly backward. I trained one carbon arc searchlight's long, tight, white beam on the moored fleet and bank, and the other on the bridge pier just ahead of the tow. I had the engines on very "Slow Bell." (Though we no longer use engine room bells, since the engines are now controlled from the pilothouse, old steamboat words are still part of our lexicon: "All Stop," "Full Ahead," "Back Her Down.") I backed on the port engine and came ahead on the starboard and used the end of the fleet as a sort of fulcrum to start the head out toward the channel. Soon the astern way (movement) stopped, and as I watched the head, a narrow gap of water opened up between the tow and the fleet. Free of restraints, we were about to be on our way. As we worked away from the fleet and started coming slow ahead on both engines, I truly realized what a monstrous thing this tow was as it stretched out into the darkness, the head slowly swinging out into clear water and toward the channel.

I was impressed with the genius of humankind, which made this whole impressive endeavor possible. And made possible control under the hands and eyes of one man. I was carried away with emotion. It was all so amazing: the silence, the darkness, the size of the tow, the many lights, which, though faint, were all known and friendly beacons to me. I was moved that I, once a puling youngster, a sometimes coward in the schoolyard, had overcome a shaky start and was actually controlling this huge floating majesty of steel and power. I was touched that some foolish human being had decided I was a man to be trusted with this job.

The twin searchlights were now focused, one each on the bridge piers. The sight as I looked out over the thousand feet of steel moving slowly away from the shore, the personal command of the powerful boat doing my bidding, my understanding of what I was doing, my growing confidence in myself—it was all so overwhelming that I actually sat there in the pilot's chair weeping. It did not seem possible that I, a 145-pound man who had known humiliation and fear, should have ever reached this exalted Olympus. But there I was, and I would be nowhere else. This was the happiest moment of my life as a full-grown man. Nothing that any other mortal was doing in the world at that time ranked, in my eyes, with what I was doing!

Soon the head was well out into the river and the stern clear of the fleet, and I started thinking of straightening her up in the river. But before it was too late to back down and get out of the way, I called for any traffic coming toward us in or above the bridges. Any southbound boat would have the right of way and could ask me to hold up below until he cleared the bridges. I would have been happy to wait. The last thing I needed on my maiden voyage was to have to pass a big tow in the sometimes narrow confines of the bridge areas.

A towboat answered my call. It was the *Orco*, northbound like us, with a full tow of coal barges.

"Cap," he said, "I just cleared the last bridge and never met anybody. Looks like it's all yours."

"Got that okay," I answered, "and thank you for answering, maybe see you up the creek a piece." I gave my call letters and completed with the message: "The *Ravenswood* northbound at the Southern Railroad Bridge. The *Ravenswood* clear."

I added power and started to straighten the tow up in the middle of the channel span. She did my bidding effortlessly on half power, and soon we were lined out half and half through the bridge, with the green channel light above us at the midpoint of the bridge splitting right down the middle of the tow. This meant we were dead on course. I put the engine levers to "full ahead," and the boat began to increase her speed to a breathtaking seven miles per hour, which she would maintain day and night. We would reach the Ashland Oil fleets at Mile 319 on schedule if we encountered no untoward lock delays, the river didn't rise, and the current did not grow stiffer.

By now we were passing the lower west end of Cincinnati, with all its industrial shore installations on the right descending bank. Soon we were up under the C&O bridge and approaching the venerable Suspension Bridge, under which the lights of downtown Cincinnati opened up to our view. The Kentucky shore was more subdued, the brightest lights being those of restaurants made from retired steamboats. We passed beautiful Riverside Drive, with only street lights showing and the houses dark, where the residents with normal jobs lay asleep.

I must admit that I was a mite nervous, and I somewhat oversteered so that the head of the tow swung from side to side like a bull facing a matador. There is a vast difference, I found, between moving one or two barges, the normal tow of a harbor tug, and pushing this vast field of steel. I learned that you planned your steering corrections well in advance and did not wait until you were on a collision course with riverside objects or bridge piers. But the tow handled with ease, and in less than an hour we had cleared the last bridge and had no wreckage bobbing around behind us. In another hour we were well above Cincinnati and its familiar lights and shapes. It commenced to get awfully dark, but things went well. This night I found the darkness a friend, for it challenged me to be unafraid.

A great joy leaped in my heart at the discovery of a new-found me. A me that I was proud of to the point of sensing a gradual expunging of past mistakes, small acts of unkindness, dishonesties, and occasional cowardice. A man's first night watch on a large tow is truly a catharsis. I found a great joy in my heart at the solitude and my new competence, a great joy in my heart for the boat, the huge docile tow, and the men sleeping peacefully below, serene in their perhaps misplaced trust in this neophyte to get them safely through the night. I felt great joy in being alone in this small, almost pitch-dark house atop a quiet world below, a world of great and tireless machines that did my bidding, and small sleeping men, who did no man's bidding unless an alarm sounded.

There is simply nothing quite like being alone in a darkened pilothouse gazing out the great front window at ephemeral lights, some your own and some on shore to steer by. It is an exciting loneliness that you would not trade for any place else in the world—cigarettes and hot coffee near at hand, gripping the steering levers with growing confidence, the room only dimly lit by the greenish yellow glow of the radar screen.

"They'll have to drag me out of here," I thought, "for I'll never go peacefully. This all belongs to me."

At 6:00 A.M., the captain came up the steps and into the pilothouse to relieve me, bringing all the mundane world with him. He was preceded by the smell of baloney, a so-called meat he was inordinately fond of. He was a veteran pilot who became a great friend and mentor, but he had one fault: he ate his beloved baloney in two-inch-thick hunks without bread—a practice that almost made me gag and that I never got used to. As I turned the levers over to him this morning, after my first night as a line-haul pilot, I was tired—but if he had asked me, I would have gladly taken on another watch.

My last duty before quitting was to fill in the logbook. I was tempted to write of all the night's experience had meant to me, but such an entry would have puzzled and confused the most sympathetic of my colleagues, not to mention the home office. Instead, I wrote only that we had covered thirty-six miles, had passed two other tows, both downbound, and that we were currently approaching Meldahl Lock, Mile 434.

The captain asked me how my first watch had gone, and I answered, "Pretty well. No problem."

Alphonse and Gaston

River pilots are often garrulous and lonely, and some use any excuse to chat with another pilot—about their hemorrhoids, their wives, their kids, their tobacco base. The radio is the conveyor of all this chitchat. I learned early on as a towboater that the radio was also sometimes used to play "Chicken"—and with a 1,200-foot tow, this game can be right dangerous.

I happened to tune in to one of these wars of nerves one day while delivering a single-tank barge to Conway, Pennsylvania. Two large tows were approaching each other from opposite directions near Pipe Creek Bend, where the river room was kind of tight. The pilots got into a typical Alphonse-Gaston routine about how they would pass; on the surface the exchange was super-deferential, but the hidden motive of each mucho-macho man was to prove his own superior nerve and total control.

I steered well clear from the jousting lists to avoid any possible flying timberheads or other barge parts; I sneaked up the West Virginia shore and listened in. The routine went something like this:

A radio voice drawls, sure of itself, "This is the *Elaine G.* calling the northbound boat coming up on Hard Scrabble Bend."

A chipper, confident voice answers, "The *J. Page Hayden* right back. Go ahead, good Cap'n." The *Hayden* pilot knows exactly why he has been called. His tow and that of the *Elaine G.* are approaching one another from opposite directions and must soon pass, with not a great deal of river room to spare. But instead of picking a side of the river on which to pass the other boat, he plays out the game.

"Why, good afternoon there, Cap. I guess that's you I'm a lookin' at coming my way. Which side would you like?"

As the downbound boat, the *Elaine G.* is the "privileged" vessel, and her pilot can name the side he wants. But that's too easy. Been me, I'd have immediately picked the one- or two-whistle side, whichever gave me the greatest margin of safety. If the other guy goes along with it and hits a submerged dike, why that's his problem.

"Shoot, Skipper, I just got this little old dab of seventeen loads," says the *J. Page Hayden.* "I can go either way that suits you best."

"Shucks, pardner, ah'm jest paddling down the middle of the creek with these twenty-one pieces." Score one for the *Elaine G.* "You just tell me where you want me, and I'll be there."

"Don't make a bit of difference to me, pard. I'm moving along pretty good and can go either way that'll make you happy."

"I gotcha okay, Cap'n." A brief pause while the *Elaine G.* pilot thinks of a way out of conceding.

All the while this dialogue was going on, two flotillas of barges with a combined size of nine acres, 12,000 horsepower and a weight of 40,000 or 50,000 tons were approaching each other on a collision course at a combined speed of sixteen to eighteen miles per hour.

Finally, "I ain't movin' all that slow," says the *Elaine G.* pilot. "I can go to either side with no trouble, and just let you slide on by whichever way you want."

"Well, Skipper . . ." A faint concession in the voice of the *J. Page Hayden* pilot—things were by now getting critical, though surrender was not yet possible. "I'm kinda shaped up for a one, and I'll just stay on it if you like. Or if not, I can swing her over and get you on the two. Whichever you'd like."

At last the two pilots are beginning to communicate, and it's about time, or there's gonna be a smash-up that will make Mount St. Helens sound like a 105 Howitzer.

"Why, one would just tickle me pink, good Cap'n. But if a two is your fancy, why, then you just take it." The *Elaine G.* senses victory.

"Well, pard, I reckon a one will do, since it suits *you* so well." The *J. Page Hayden* almost pulls victory from the jaws of defeat. "So a one is what she'll be." But he does not quite win, because he did pick a definite side before the *Elaine G.* did.

As the two tows passed, each pilot came out of the bridge of his boat and waved both arms over his head in the traditional salute of rivermen. But the pilot on the *Elaine G.* waved ever so slightly more vigorously, for he knew that he had come out best in the war of nerves.

I breathed a sigh of relief as the two behemoths passed safely, amazed that these guys always seem to make it. I have never heard that last-second transmission before two stubborn pilots combine tows head-on and go off the air forever. They would go down dueling, I suppose, something like this: "Well, you damn fool, I gave you your choice, whyn't you take it?" "Why, you stupid crackpot, you were the downbound boat, why didn't you tell me what side you wanted?"

These encounters taught me a lot: to keep my dealings with others cooperative and nonconfrontational and never to think that river people, just because their grammar isn't so good, are unsubtle or simple.

Coffee, the Real Lubricant

If any boat I ran was not equipped with a coffee-making device in the pilothouse, my first act would be to requisition one. If turned down by the company, I would provide my own and leave it aboard until I was no longer associated with the vessel. Coffee was a necessity for keeping my cool. It was not unusual for me, in a six-hour watch, to go through an eight-cup percolator (along with at least one and a half packs of the old-fashioned nonfiltered lung busters of yesteryear).

If I were to get caught during a lock approach or difficult string of bridges without coffee, the whole crew had best abandon ship, for catastrophe was nigh! There have been times when the head of a 105-foot-wide tow about to enter a 110-foot-wide lock chamber would find me not steering a vessel but scurrying all over it looking for tobacco and caffeine. This, of course, is why today my circulatory system looks like the inside of a century-old iron water pipe.

Not only was the coffee pot as important as the fuel tank, no doubt about it, but I wanted it right there beside me in the pilothouse. I did not like to have deckhands constantly running up to the pilothouse with a fresh cup. That is not what deckhands are paid to do. Further, coffee carried from the galley was usually cold and half-slopped out of the cup by the time it arrived. It also took time to teach a new man how I liked my coffee and time for me to get accustomed to a new-flavored thumb. The men were willing enough to bring me coffee, knowing I was busy steering the boat, but they invariably forgot to take the empty cups back to the galley, and by the end of a watch the galley was stripped of cups and the pilothouse looked like a badly managed scullery in a short-order restaurant.

I do have to admit, however, that having the coffee brought to the pilothouse served a number of important functions. Just as it fueled the pilot, it oiled interpersonal relations. For one thing, it demonstrated that the deckhand in question was busy, busy, busy, like the White Rabbit, and that he just happened to be passing by with a cup in his hands while making his way from one job to another. Sometimes it worked. For I admit to occasionally being guilty of sitting up in the pilothouse coffeeless and alone and, in my loneliness, conjuring up make-work because I knew my crew was sitting down in the galley reading *Playboy* and eating ice cream and cake.

Or the deckhand's offering might be made out of sympathy for the loneliness of the pilot, respect for the pilot's having reached his professional plateau, and sometimes, with a new man, sheer awe of his skills. I will never forget the night I visited my first dark pilothouse, bearing a cup of coffee, thinking to purchase with it a temporary seat on Olympus. God, I was impressed. It was pitch dark inside the pilothouse and out except for the faint glow of the instruments and the yellowish green of the radar screen. The great bulk of the pilot almost blended in with the dark but still emerged as a dim silhouette illuminated in front by the instrument lights.

The man stood up and gazed into the radar, his face yellowish green and strong and all-knowing. Fairly quivering with awe, I handed him the coffee. He reached out his hand, not deigning to look, knowing with imperious sureness that the cup would be placed there and that when he put it to his lips they would meet with the drinking edge and not the handle. He said, "Thanks," nothing more, and certainly there was no encouragement to stay and chat. I stayed anyway, making myself small and quiet, watching this minor god busting through the impenetrable dark with a huge tow of fifteen loaded barges.

The ubiquitous cup of coffee could also be a peacemaking symbol. If the tow work had not gone well and this was patently the fault of the crew or a particular crew member and as pilot or captain I had expressed displeasure, then, when the work was done, the guilty one or a representative of the guilty ones would appear with a cup of coffee and a certain contriteness of manner. If I was understanding and the mistakes had not been repeated, I would recognize the coffee for what it represented, accept it, make its bearer welcome, and indicate that the incident was forgotten by not mentioning it. These were fine moments.

If I was the one who had performed badly, when I knew that I had been inept and caused everyone extra work, then I would make the overtures. I could not abandon the tow and trot to the galley with four hot cups, but I would call the galley and request coffee. When it arrived, usually by way of the mate, I would contrive contriteness in my voice and sort of apologize by semi-admitting that the recent poor boat handling was all my fault. "By golly, Roy, I just couldn't get that damn barge to flank over there where you wanted it," I might say, letting the barge take some of the blame but really meaning that I was having one of those watches when I couldn't do anything right.

The mate might answer, recognizing and accepting the apology, "No problem, Cap, we got her in there all right." If he was feeling especially expansive and forgiving, he might add, "Besides, I was watching the wheelwash and it seemed like that starboard propeller ain't puttin' out like it ought." Sweet boy, I could kiss him. These too were fine moments.

Any professional riverman, whether he's in the pilothouse or on deck, knows that there are days when he can't, as dear old Daddy said, "pour piss out of a boot," even with written instructions. But if he is mostly proficient, he will shrug off—with the simple commandment "Judge not harshly, lest ye be judged"—those days when turning the boot upside down never occurs to him. Coffee, not oil, makes those fine moments possible.

Pride Goeth
before a Bellyache

There are lots of skills to master in towboating, none more important than dealing with the people on board. The crew becomes like a family, with the captain as father and head. I found myself faced by the same kind of problems as on shore. Like in the case of Ol' John.

John wasn't the best deckhand in the world, and he wasn't the worst, but he was the oldest both in years and seniority on one boat I ran. He was the classic mountain man, a taciturn, opinionated, suspicious, "hate the company—love the union," "I know my rights" sort of guy. He was of Scotch-English ancestry, and the kind of man that made the early Britons among the world's toughest fighters and most difficult people to govern. He was resentful of authority, and as much for that reason as for his love for the finished product, had cooked off more than a little "shine" in his time. He and I got along pretty well, but if John felt affronted, he would kind of quiver his jaw muscles, squint down his eyes, shift his "chaw," and tell you what you could do with your boat and your job.

If his honor was sullied, he'd revert to the "code of the hills," which says that a punch in the nose is not sufficient satisfaction; only a gun or a knife can restore a man's honor. And there ain't nothin' in the code that says you gotta be lookin' your man in the eye when you do him in. That was Ol' John, who in one incident was his own worst enemy.

Depending on the whim of the captain, the seating arrangements at meal time can be strictly formalized or, except for the captain's place, on a first come, first served basis. Being a democratic sort of fellow, provided that no one usurped my place, I allowed crew members to sit where they pleased. But this rule didn't apply to John. He was a firm believer in seniority, and as the senior deckhand he always ate at the same place. We all liked John, and because his insistence on this minor recognition was no big deal, we indulged him in it.

One evening about 5:45, the forward watch was eating dinner preparatory to going to work at six. John had not yet put in an appearance, and we had a new man aboard. He sat down in John's place and commenced shoveling it in. I didn't say anything to him, expecting he'd finish before John got there and figuring to mention that one inviolate seat to him later on. He was a big, good-natured sort, and I expected no problem in explaining this one taboo aboard the boat.

But John walked in and saw this foreign body at his place. The outrage on his face was hilarious, but because none of us knew what was going to happen, we just stared down at our plates and kept eating. Not so the new man; he looked up with a mouthful of mashed potatoes and roast pork, waved his fork, and managed a cheerful, "Howdy, pardner, be done here in a minute." But the damage was done. John's pride was sticking out all over him, and he wouldn't have sat in that place now even if the other feller had jumped up and thrown himself overboard. He just stomped over to the pot, got a cup of coffee, and left the galley, his anger reflected in the slam of the screen door. So he missed that meal.

Well, the crew thought this was funny, and so did I. If I'd done the right thing by John, I would have straightened the new man out right then, but I didn't. I was as curious as everybody else to see what was going to happen. And John was so cussed stubborn and so prideful I just didn't feel inclined to do anything right off.

The same thing happened at breakfast the next morning and then again at lunch and dinner. Every time John came in the galley, that boy would be wolfing it down and would unfailingly greet him with a cheerful word and an assurance that he'd be "done here right soon." And each time Ol' John would just grab a cup of coffee and stalk out.

After his evening disappearing act, the new man said, "That ol' boy don't eat much, does he?" This about broke us up, and we all agreed that John seemed to be off his feed a mite.

Now, John could have solved the problem himself by asking me to straighten out the new hand, but he was just plain too ornery and stubborn. He could have showed up five minutes sooner, but he was a punctual man, used to sitting down exactly fifteen minutes before the hours, not one second before or after, and he'd be darned if he would change. Far as he was concerned, when he walked in that galley, his chair was supposed to be empty and waiting for him. He had his rights, by God!

Well, this went on for a couple of days, and John kept missing meals. Before long he commenced slowing down and dragging around like he had a bad case of the punies. So I decided it was time to straighten things out. I asked him what his problem was, acting as though I thought he was half sick but knowing full well that he was half starved and plumb put out about the usurper at the dinner table. I had my answer all ready. I'd say, "Well, darn, John, I'm shore sorry about that; it never occurred to me. I'll tell that new feller about it tonight."

But John surprised me. "Cap," he said, "I'm so all-fired constipated I cain't hardly stand up straight."

I had expected almost any kind of answer but that. How could a man who had apparently not eaten in three days be constipated? I told him to take a bunch of Ex-Lax and give 'er another try in a few hours, and he said he would.

Later that evening I explained the situation to the new man, and he said, "Why, shoot, Cap, it don't matter to me where I sit long's it's near the food."

Soon after that I had another visitor in the pilothouse. It was the cook. "Cap," he said, "either I ain't feedin' these guys enough or we got some of the biggest mice afloat on this boat."

"How's that, Mr. Cook?" I asked.

"Well, sir," he replied, "there's a whole stick of baloney missing, a coupla two-pound boxes of cheese, and three loaves of fresh bread."

I really had to laugh at that. It sure wasn't mice or a mystery to me where the missing vittles had gone. And it was no wonder poor Ol' John couldn't stand up straight. Four pounds of cheese and three loaves of bread would constipate a bull elephant!

Well, I reckon everything came out all right for John during the night, because at 5:45 A.M. he walked into the galley and took his rightful place, and from the look on his face you'd never guess that anything had ever been otherwise.

Little Cat Feet?

The pilothouse was almost pitch dark, the only light a faint glow from the instruments and an eerie greenish emanation that came from the round face of the radarscope. We were downbound in a shutout fog.

I was alone, for I did not encourage company or distracting chatter under such conditions. I was at ease. My body slouched in the pilot's chair just as it did during most of the two six-hour watches I stood each working day. I smoked a cigarette and sipped a cup of coffee, but my mind had sort of dissolved into the vessel. There were no random thoughts flitting through it. It was clear and attuned to what I was doing.

On a normal dark night this state of affairs did not pertain. During a daylight watch it did not happen, but when I was required to navigate in dense fog, it did. I could not see four feet in front of me. Only muted sounds intruded in an otherwise silent world, for the fog absorbed sound just as it swallowed up all light and visual references. My world was like a small spaceship hurtling through the interstellar void, for all the reference there was to an outside reality or to the sensation of movement.

The radio crackled and groaned on low volume. I would have liked to turn it off, but did not dare, for I must above all things monitor other traffic. Through the pilothouse terminal of a speaker connected to another on the bow, I could hear things like the faint chug of a small engine, a distant human cry, a muffled fog bell or boat whistle. What usually came through was a strange and occult gibberish as it monitored with electronic ears the opaque world of the riverbanks, both ahead and alongside the tow.

Now, as the great steel bows of the barges bore through the dark and clinging murk, I could distinguish the swish of the bow wave, the creak and strain of taut rigging wires, the thud of a log swept under the tow as it bumped its way aft, an occasional bird cry, and the flutter of the company flag that rode on the head of the tow. There were also strange and unidentifiable sounds, squeaks and moans, shrill squeals, and one could swear on occasion that there was a muted whispering and the sound of unearthly wings. That, of course, was all imagination . . . wasn't it?

My mind in its apparent abandonment of my body had left all systems on automatic—breathing, swallowing, muscular function. The one sense I consciously controlled was my vision. There was nothing to see outside—only gray, moist nothingness—and only darkness within, but two vital instruments claimed my eyes' attention: the radarscope and the swing meter. With these twin miracles, plus concentration and experience, I could safely navigate a gigantic vessel down a relatively narrow and twisting river; I could make locks, some bridges, and could pass other vessels of the same size as mine with ease.

The radarscope was surrounded by adjustment knobs for brightness, gain (sharpness of picture), anti-sea clutter, bearing or angle of approach, range (the distance of objects coming up on my stern or ahead of me), and peripheral lighting. In the center of the round scope was a bright dot. This was me. Extending forward was an inch-long white streak. That was my tow. Trailing behind was a small clutter of blips that represented the wake. I could see those blips change in accordance with rudder angles of attack. From the top of the scope to the bottom, dead center, and passing through the length of our own image, was the thin white sailing line. From the center dot emanated a bright, tight beam of light that extended to the edge of the screen and constantly rotated in a clockwise direction around the face of the scope. This was the sweep or header flash, and was an electronic picture of the radio waves transmitted by the revolving antennae atop the pilothouse. As it revolved, it displayed the shape of the riverbanks, both ahead and behind, as well as any obstacle in our path, like, for instance, another towboat.

The swing meter, a small back box with a dimly lit dial, told me electronically even in this fog what my eyes would tell me in daylight, namely how fast the tow head was steering, and when, as indicated by the radar display, to start bringing her back on straight rudder once on the desired new course.

The name of the game in blind navigating was that the two instruments be synchronized (this was done in daytime when I could see that the swing meter and radar were not lying to me), that I know the river, that I concentrate totally on what I was doing, and that I have confidence in electronics. Many humans in my day were not programmed to trust anything but their eyes; placing one's confidence in a little black needle and what was to a novice a greenish blob took some getting used to. Many pilots I knew lacked this confidence and would tie up at the first sign of fog, aware that a mishap could mean losing their license. Even the Coast Guard viewed radar only as an aid to navigation, to be used just long enough to get into safe harbor or a convenient tie-off. They did not forbid us to navigate on radar, but if we elected to do so and caused an accident, we would be in serious trouble. The companies that we worked for, however, liked pilots to keep going in fog. Tying off meant lost revenue and higher operating costs.

I always enjoyed navigating by radar and other electronic aids, confronting a constantly changing series of problems. On such a watch I was doing something that darn few other people in the world could do and, best of all, it made those six long hours go by in a hurry. When they were over and my body and mind became one again, I would be really wrung out, and the old bunk was the only cure.

Ninety-Five Percent Boredom, Five Percent Pure Terror

Quincey Bend, just above Walker Landing Light and stretching five miles to Buena Vista, Ohio (called Booney Vista on the river), is an easy place to navigate, almost no bend at all. Ordinarily, it would give a pilot not a moment's care. In fact, I viewed its width and gentle effortless sweep with great affection and appreciation.

I was coming to this comfortable steer at about three o'clock one morning, downbound with a tow of mixed petroleum products. The river was high, the current was fast, and we were booming along at about twelve miles per hour in a shut-out fog. I couldn't even see the handrail around the pilothouse. It had been strictly a radar watch since leaving Greenup Lock at one o'clock, but, as I've said, I rather liked running on radar. I was feeling pretty good about the whole thing. My relief was awaiting me when we got to Cincinnati the next afternoon, and I had already gotten through the Sciotoville Bridge and the Portsmouth Bridge in grand style.

I had talked to the oncoming boat whose furry and caterpillar-like facsimile was already displayed on the radar screen, and we had agreed on a one-whistle passing. Soon, as we drew closer, his image would undergo an electronic metamorphosis and he would elongate and narrow and more nearly resemble what he was, a thousand-foot-long, fifteen-barge coal tow. There was plenty of river room for us both. Life was good. All was well inside my small, cubed universe that was devoid of light except for the faint glow of the instruments and the greenish face of the radar screen.

It was pretty cold outside, though, and the small battered electric heater we used for a foot warmer was going full blast. I reached for my coffee cup but did not quite make it—there was a sudden ZZZing noise from the heater, and great clouds of smoke erupted from the pilothouse walls. The dense smoke of burning insulation immediately filled the air. It is a dangerous, choking, lung-searing smoke that must chemically kill even before death comes by asphyxiation. The insulation from all the 110-volt circuitry must have broken down its chemical bonds all at once. My serene and placid little universe filled with opaque and noxious gases like those of some exploding supernova, and suddenly I became a choking, terrified mortal, and no longer the serene man in control.

My first instinct was to run for the door and into the pure and fresh night air that my poisoned and outraged lungs demanded. Then I remembered where I was and what was taking place elsewhere than in this deadly pilothouse. I pulled the throttles to idle ahead and ran out the door anyway. What matter if this 15,000-ton mass was careening down the river, for the moment blind and unguided because no human hand triggered its hydraulic synapses? Better it should run unleashed awhile than lose its small human master who interpreted what its electronic eye perceived and gave direction and purpose to its mindless rush through the opaque void. For this great steel beast's purposes, a dead pilot would be worse than a temporarily absent one. Besides, I found being dead an intolerable idea. I wanted out. I wanted to live.

I breathed deeply, once, twice; it was very painful. That was no natural combustion in there. That was a poison gas. God and science alone knew what artful couplings of toxic chemicals went into that insulation. I alone felt how eager they were to be released from their bondage by fire and to return to their original state as a gas or a liquid, not as a solid.

I propped open the starboard door and rushed around to the port side to do the same there to create a cross draft. This would help, but not enough. I must get the front window open. Taking a deep breath and closing my eyes, I plunged back into the murky depth of the room. The smoke pierced the veils of my eyelids; it was blinding and acrid, and my eyes watered fiercely, but familiarity with my space got me to the window. The smoke, though somewhat diminished, was still pouring from the walls. I kicked the malfunctioning heater away, breaking the cord. I flung open the window. Thank heaven it was one that opened easily, not one of those that surrender only to an axe. I had to replenish my air.

I was unable to see the radar through the smoke, but I remembered that we had been nearly on straight rudder when the smoke began. If I hadn't inadvertently moved the rudders in my flight to get air, we should be quite safe for a few more precious moments at this reduced speed and in this sweet and gentle bend. I could only hope that everything remained as it was before. If this had happened in one of those really vicious switchbacks that the Ohio is known for, we would have been in deep shit and I would have long since hit the general alarm.

In a bad turn the tow would have hurled itself against something immovable and we would have had loose petroleum barges all over the river, running free in total fog. A boat that is "loose headed" is no more than a minute blip on the radar; its direction and the angle of attack needed to corral a barge can be determined only by close study at the cost of precious seconds. You try mightily to pierce the opaque whiteness to locate the runaway and determine whether you are in a position to catch it or whether you had better get the hell out of the way. All of a sudden, that huge creature might begin to show itself, vaguely, briefly. Then it may disappear again. It is out there somewhere close by, but its speed and its lay are impossible to gauge.

Smoke was pouring out of the open doors and the front window now. The paneling in the pilothouse was fire resistant, and the outer skin was steel. There was not much fear of fire, but it would be foolhardy to assume there was no danger of it. There was no way of knowing what was inside the walls, and "where there's smoke . . ." At the moment, I wanted only for the fumes to abate so that I could live long enough to do the things I must do. I found what I was looking for: the ship intercom system and the button for the galley. I knew from long practice where that button was, and I knew that at 3:00 A.M. the crew would be there, and they were. If they hadn't been, I would have hit the general alarm in order to alert them to danger.

"I've got a bad electrical fire up here," I announced. I spoke quietly. This was no time to communicate panic. "One of you get up here on the double with a fire extinguisher. Stand by a second." I dashed out onto the deck for air. The pilothouse air was not as bad as it had been but was still unbreathable. After a deep lungful, I returned to the controls. "Okay, one of you head for the engine room. Tell the chief the fire is in the 110-volt circuits; maybe he has a circuit breaker for just that. Wait." I started to cough. "Stand by a second." I plunged outdoors once more, then back in to the intercom again.

"Tell him if he is not sure, to just wait for further word." I did not want the radio or radar inadvertently turned off. "Then head back to the galley. I'll advise you whether to wake the rest of the crew."

I had two more jobs to do. I must let the oncoming boat know of possible danger, and I must get a good look at that radarscope to see if the danger of collision was becoming an actuality.

The deckhand arrived on the bridge, where I had retreated once more. "Lord a mercy," he exclaimed, seeing the smoke roiling out the window and doors. "Yeah," I answered. "Just set that extinguisher down. I don't think we're going to need it. Then head for the galley and bring up that big floor fan and an extension cord. There's nothing you can do up here now."

Breathing deeply first, I reentered the pilothouse, grabbed the radio hand mike attached to its curlycued cord, and tossed it gently out the front window. Exiting, I retrieved it, gave my call sign and vessel name, and the name of the other boat in my transmission. I did not transmit "Mayday." There was no need for that, at least not yet, and I hoped there would be none. Besides, I would feel awkward and melodramatic saying the words. If the typical riverman were standing in the pilothouse with water up around his neck, he would do little more than drawl something like, "Well, pard, seems like I got me a leetle problem here. This ol' boat's got right smart more water in her than she should have. You reckon you could kinda mosey over this way and maybe give us a hand?"

To my call, the pilot of the oncoming boat said, "The *Orco* back. Go ahead, Captain." In spite of my allegiance to "cool," I thought, what's wrong with this guy? Couldn't he see the smoke pouring out of this wreck? Then I realized that the fog had made all this my own totally private drama. No one in the world had been witness to my frantic scurrying; no one could see the ominous clouds coming out the window or smell the searing fumes. Not even God could pierce this damp white veil that so totally shut out my little piece of the world.

"Skipper, I got a bad electrical fire in the pilothouse," I said to the *Orco*'s pilot, "no flames as yet, but Lordy is it smoky! I've got her pulled back, but I figgered I better let you know in case your screen shows us a-headin' your way."

"The *Orco* back. Yeaaah . . ." He kind of strung it out, and I knew that he was checking his scope. "Gotcha okay. Don't appear nothing's changed on my picture. We'll be passing right soon anyhow. Looks pretty good to me. How bad is your fire? Anything we can do?"

"Naw, Skipper. I reckon we're gonna be all right. I don't figger we'll get any fire; she's just smoky, and that insulation is fit to strangle a man, but it's clearing up some now. Gimme a kick back if anything changes. I got a fan coming up. I'd sure like to get a look at that radar, though. Kinda makes a feller feel better when he knows where he's going."

"Lord, yes," he chortled, sounding tickled pink at my little witticism. "I know what you mean. Well, okay, pard, we'll watch 'er. Gimme a holler if you need any help."

"Will do, captain, will do and thanks. Have a good trip on up." I cleared the air.

"Got that okay, pard, same to you." He gave his call letters. "The *Orco*, clear."

I had been standing on the deck throughout this conversation and now plunged once again into the pilothouse. The fan was doing its work. The room was still smoky and noxious, but one could survive. I punched the galley button. "Okay, all under control. Ask the chief to come up."

It was all over. The smoke was clearing well, and I could see the radar and determine that we were still on course. I was glad I had not sounded the general alarm. Men grumbly and sleepy would just now be returning to their beds. I would not care about their grumbles; nobody guaranteed them uninterrupted sleep when they chose this life, but I had affection for them and was glad that I hadn't had to disturb them.

In half an hour it was business as usual in the pilothouse, only colder without my heater. That particular jury-rigged foot warmer would cause no more trouble, for in the excitement, I had managed to see that it went over the side.

A deckhand brought me a cup of hot coffee. It was fresh and good, and this time I got to drink it. My little universe was once again serene, if a mite smelly. We proceeded downriver, nothing and no one but me and the insulation any the worse for wear. The deckhands and the engineer sat on the lounge behind me talking over the night's excitement. The chief was already relegating my adventure to minor status with his account of an engine room fire, one that "shore was a *real* 'far.'"

That's Showbiz, Jack

There were days as a pilot when I couldn't hit the riverbank if I steered for it. On such days the boat was cantankerous and lazy; the mate was the same and seemed to have gone blind and speechless as well. The river had a whole new set of outdrafts and mud humps where none used to be. And then there were days when I could do no wrong. If called upon to do so, I could put a 100-foot-wide tow into a 50-foot-wide lock chamber. Most pilots have both kinds of days. When it's the good kind, brother, do you ever feel great—especially if you have an

The Markland Locks and Dam at Markland, Indiana, downriver from Cincinnati. The job is to guide the gargantuan tow into the chamber, where the water is raised or lowered, allowing the boat and barges to enter another level of the river. No wonder Jack wanted to show off a little (courtesy of Corps of Engineers, Louisville, Kentucky).

audience! The temptation to show off is strong. Especially at a lock, where there are onlookers. I never did anything too foolish to impress the crowd, but who knows what dumb stuff I might have done if I had not had the example of a good friend of mine named Jack Hicks.

Ol' Jack was having one of those good days. He was making a downbound lockage at Meldahl Lock and had a chamber full: a tow 1,180 feet long and 108 feet wide, all petroleum loads. It was a lovely summer Sunday afternoon, and he had a sizable audience of lock visitors hanging over the fence on the observers' platform, including the inevitable flock of pretty girls. Well, things were just going royally for old Jack. He had made a beautiful approach, then greased that herd in as pretty as you please. It all went so well that he was in a state of euphoria, and with the call "All clear the bull nose," which means the tow head is in the chamber, he really relaxed and started playing to the crowd, especially the girls, forgetting that his work was not done.

But when things are going that well, you've just got to give the crowd a look at the man responsible for it all. After all, there are the girls, and you sure wouldn't want to deprive those with cameras of capturing you on film. It would be unseemly to emerge from the pilothouse bowing

McAlpine Locks and Dam at Louisville. To the right are a towboat and barges in a 1,200-foot chamber (a full tow would have less room to spare); to the left, a chamber 600 feet in length (courtesy of Corps of Engineers, Louisville, Kentucky)

A full tow of fifteen barges (as seen from the boat), 1,150 feet long and 105 feet wide, in a lock chamber 1200 by 110 feet. A tight squeeze!

and blowing kisses. On the other hand, the ego won't let you stay confined in the pilothouse where no mortal or, more specifically, adoring female eye can reach.

Well, the usual ploy to get yourself out of there with some dignity is to walk out on the bridge, head level if not down (one never acknowledges the crowd and is always the complete professional), then glance toward the stern as if something there needs looking into, something that only your keen eye can detect. Then you look toward the bow, eyes squinted like Clint Eastwood's, before checking the stern once more. To the deckhand back there you voice some stupid command like "Be sure you get a good tight line on 'er, Joe," which cannot be heard by the audience but certainly seems commanding and captain-like. With that brief appearance before your public, you retire to the mysterious cubicle with all those dials, radios, levers, and throttles that only you can understand

and make do your bidding. Then, perhaps, you make a slight, totally unnecessary adjustment to the port throttle, which causes a dramatic bit of smoke to rise from the idling engine. This buys you another trip to the bridge to satisfy yourself that the all-important adjustment has accomplished its purpose.

Brother Hicks pretty well tried all these devices, playing to the crowd for all he was worth. His tow was moving well, slowly, and on the wall (it had only two feet to shift around in), and except for engine changes the rest of the lockage was up to the mate. This conscientious soul was down on the head of the tow, deep in the lock chamber and out of the limelight. When the barges were in the correct position, he ordered over the old-fashioned two-way loudspeaker, "All stop, Jack." But old John Wayne Hicks was too busy hamming it up to hear him.

The mate, no doubt assuming that his order had been carried out, continued his mental calculations of speed and distance, and came up with the wrong answers. The numbers on the lock wall were passing him by just as fast as ever. "Well, she's all stopped," he must have said to himself, "and not slowing down. Better back 'er down a little." He called to the pilothouse, "Roll 'er back a little, Jack."

By now, Jack had given up all semblance of being a pilot; the limelight had proved too much for him. He was winking and waving and having a ball.

Meanwhile, the massive lower gate was getting bigger and bigger from the mate's point of view, and the man was sounding downright frantic. "What the hell's the matter with this boat?" he yelled out. He hollered over the speaker, "Take her back hard, Jack," but the good captain paid him no mind.

The tow still did not slow down, and the mate could see that they were going to hit the gate. More than a little helpless, he looked up at the pilothouse, and there was the prince of players standing on the bridge, waving and carrying on something fierce.

That did it for the mate. At the top of his amplified voice, he bellowed, "Jack, you silly son of a bitch, stop showing off and back this God damn mess down." Over the loudspeaker his words could be heard in Cincinnati, not to mention on the observation platform, where it could be heard by the local onlookers, pretty girls and all. Jack, suddenly brought to his senses by this undignified affront to his role as a star, leaped to the controls and horsed the engines to full astern. But it was too late.

"Wham!" That tow plowed into the lower gate, bounced back, and appeared to sort of shake its head like a bull run into a freight train. The

Spectators at a lock

deckhand on the stern flew off the timberhead he was sitting on and landed on the deck, looking all bewildered. The mate staggered and almost fell over the head of the tow, and Jack sailed about halfway out the front window of the pilothouse. Lord knows what happened to all the unsuspecting bodies down below—like the cook, the off-watch sleeping crew, and anyone unfortunate enough to be sitting on the john. He would have wound up sailing head first into the shower stall.

After the collision, silence reigned for a moment over the whole scene. Then smiles began to appear in the audience, then chuckles, then laughter, and the pretty girls seemed to laugh loudest of all. The lock crew rushed to the gate, wearing worried looks, and the lockmaster boomed out over his loud speaker, "Get that man's name, address, who he works for, and his pilot's license number."

Fortunately, the lock gate was undamaged, and the lockage returned to routine. But it was all too much for poor old Jack. He took no more bows, stayed in the pilothouse with the doors closed and as far away from the windows as possible.

Ah, how ephemeral is fame. How fast and how far the mighty fall. How cruel the fickle public! "All ah wisht," Jack later said, "was that the God damn boat had sunk right there with me on it. If I coulda figgered out a way to crawl under the instrument console and steer her from there, ah woulda shore done it."

Well, ol' Jack can take solace in the surety that even John Wayne must have fallen off his horse once in a while. Of course, the Duke could always demand a retake. I myself tried to stay out of show business and tend to the tow business.

Night Lights

I switched the radar to "on," for darkness was falling, and the river was black as the Styx at night. On the stretch I was navigating, however, it turned out that I needed it barely at all: while Mother Nature had decreed that now was time for darkness, man had decreed that in this part of the world at least the forces of darkness should hold no sway. Light came from all directions; both banks of the river were visible. Ahead the sky was illuminated by the millionfold candlepower of Pittsburgh some twelve miles upstream.

The greatest intensity and variety of lights was to the port, for there were more small communities on that bank than on the opposite shore: Freedom, Conway, Baden, Ambridge, Leetsdale. But by far the more spectacular lighting was to the starboard. We were in steel-producing country; the occasional but sudden and vivid flareups, like sunspots, of the molten "steel pours" or the dumping of still-molten slag, would light the sky and the river and tow before me in an intermittent, lurid red glow. Then it would fade for a while until the small, mortal Vulcans working the plants on the starboard bank could bring another potful to boil.

In the intervals between those volcano-like eruptions, the more vulgar light of man the merchant, the purveyor of goods and services, on our port side, took over. There was an insulting, commonplace quality about the light that guided me from that bank, a light that was ill-suited to the drama of the darkened pilothouse, the immense vessel beneath, and fifteen petroleum barges ahead of me making faint bow waves on the dark surface of the river, the tow being propelled inexorably to its destination—where its precious cargo of energy would illuminate and maintain much of the night's activity, both heroic and mundane.

I resented the intrusion of those callow and mercantile lights that constantly reminded me of my petty wants: "Cold Beer," "Steaks and Chops," Cigarettes." Hotels, motels, all-night markets, and used-car dealers vied for my attention and dollars. The traffic lights and railroad semaphores flashed "Stop" and "Go." I wanted to be free of such things, to be part of man's more heroic life.

I rescinded the primordial order and said instead, "Let there be darkness. Wink out! Collective candle power of mundane pursuits; leave me in a darkness that is dispelled only when those Titans on my starboard bank release their occasional, exultant, sky-lighting bursts of energy. Let me think this night not of man the bartender or the used-car salesman but of man the tenacious, intelligent biped, who has wrung from his own mind the knowledge to turn the resources that he has mined from the earth to his own use."

I admitted that man had not always used the earth wisely, as the environmentalists were telling us and our own eyes confirmed. But his actions were inevitable, I thought: man can no more stop the utilization or, if you will, the plundering of this minor planet's resources than he can stop the questing of the mind or the production of babies. And it is arguable that he should; man the animal is a survivor before he is a poet. The first cell that contained within it the impulse to become a man did not ask for the privilege of being. Something pushed the button marked "start," and the steady flow of imperfect, imperiously determined-to-survive creatures was set in motion. There is no button marked "stop."

So in the pilothouse that night, in a place so conducive to thinking grand thoughts of man the hero, man the harnesser of elemental powers, not man the merchant or consumer, I resented the brash and petty lights to the port side of my boat. My face was centered forward, and during the hiatuses of starboard activity, my face was half in light, half in darkness, and I thought that to an onlooker the port side of my face must appear pale and unhealthy as I awaited breathlessly for the next steel-producing eruption. When it came, the starboard side of my face would be briefly lit, darkly red, highlighted, and strong. No longer was it pasty white from the mad optician's chart of neon enticements appealing to my petty wants. It would be saturnine, now lighted, now shadowed, now darkened, the face of man the steersman of great vessels, the pourer of vast ingots, the determined accepter of the challenge laid on him at the push of the button marked "start."

But I could not have the night as I wanted it; my reversed primordial order was ignored. The port side lights stayed on, and I, the victim of petty wants, must, in order to satisfy them, keep pushing our cargo of now benign but energy-packed liquids to their destination—for when their molecular bonds were broken they would maintain that light which repelled me. But that was the way it must be. I was only a committee of one voting for darkness to the left and a continuance of the Wagnerian forging to the right. I was outvoted by the thousands of people who find happiness in the bright and artificial light so necessary to tending the store.

And truth to tell, despite the philosophical musings of that fine evening, at the end of my tour on the boat those brash lights would not be nearly so repugnant. That ugly, vulgar, flashing sign that says "Cold Beer" becomes a friendly beacon when the inner man screams to escape into the comfort of bright lights and cities and people.

Burial at Sea

We had just arrived in Cincinnati, downbound from Ashland with an eleven-barge tow of petroleum products. Some of these were to be left there, and the rest would go to Louisville. After making the main tow secure, we were responsible for delivering the local barges for discharge and retrieving them when they were empty. This we had done except for one that awaited dock space at a nearby oil company.

The boat was tied off at a barge fleeting and tug facility, and we were standing by, awaiting orders. I was running pilot on that boat, was off watch and swapping lies with the captain in the pilothouse. It was about 8:00 P.M. We were talking about the fairer sex at the time because we had both been on duty for twenty-two days, and that subject was occupying more and more of our waking hours. The captain was just getting into a whopper about a lady he had met in a bar in Charleston, West Virginia, when the radio, which had been quietly muttering to itself, suddenly hawked up some electronic phlegm, and a voice said, "They're ready for that barge down at the terminal now."

The captain picked up the hand mike, gave the boat's call letters, and replied, "Got that okay. Tell 'em we're on the way. Be there in about forty-five minutes." Then he punched the galley button on the boat's intercom and said, "All right, fellers, turn 'er loose." They untied our boat from the landing and we headed to our tow moored across the river.

Well, the captain was going to be too busy for a while to finish his tale, so I decided to demonstrate how democratic I was by going down and mingling with the crew while they wired the boat up to the barge and prepared to get under way. Of course, if it had been wintertime, there wouldn't have been enough democratic spirit in me to get me out of a warm pilothouse. But it was a pleasant summer evening. My presence on deck especially pleased Ol' John, the lead deckhand, because he always did figure that pilothouse people had the big head.

The captain eased the boat down on the barge real easy like, and as soon as the towing knees touched it, the crew commenced to putting on the face wires, the big, heavy steel cables that hold the boat to the barge. John tightened them up with the massive winches mounted on the fore deck of the boat. Me? I was not doing anything special, just standing around drinking a cup of coffee, when suddenly John let out a howl and a string of unprintable words.

I turned and saw that he was holding real hard onto his left hand with his right, looking kind of white around the eyes and ears. I saw why. Where half his left index finger used to be was now empty space. When he was cranking up the starboard winch, he had reached in to unkink the cable and had gotten that finger into the gears. Now, those gears are real slow-moving, but they are mighty big, and it sure would take a lot more than John's finger to stop them.

Being experienced in these matters (I got half a left thumb lopped off by a sharp blade myself), I said to John, "Just take it easy because it ain't gonna hurt for a while yet. Hold it real tight and *don't* look at it!" And that's good advice if you ever get a piece of yourself suddenly severed. Jump around and holler and cuss if it makes you feel better, but don't ever look at it. I made the mistake of looking at my thumb stub and almost fainted.

I called up to the captain over the intercom and told him what had happened. He radioed the harbor and had them call an ambulance, while the crew and I continued to throw off the wires. John sat on a capstan, bleeding a bit, holding tight, and cussing a little now and then—but definitely not looking at the empty space that his finger used to call home.

Soon we were back at the dock and walking Ol' John up the hill to the ambulance, just joking it up and patting him on the back and telling him how bad the novocaine needles hurt and so on—you know, just trying to cheer him up a little. But John, he wasn't laughing, only gritting his teeth. We agreed he never did have much sense of humor.

Well, after that we packed up John's things, left them at the dock, and delivered our barge. At eleven the next morning we were ready to gather up our southbound tow and head for Louisville. Just before we left, John's replacement came on board. He was the kind of fellow our barge company was so good at hiring: young and green. He showed up with nothing but the clothes he was standing in. No hat, no gloves, no sweater or work clothes, just a pair of honky-tonk shoes, a wrinkled suit the Goodwill would turn down, and a fancy cowboy shirt. I didn't doubt that he had cut a fancy figure at whatever bar he spent the night in, but it was obvious this morning that he came on board prepared to eat, sleep, and do darn little else.

The captain was facing the boat down on the tow, and once again I was on the foredeck. Not being democratic this time, but just helping out on account of the new man. We'd found him a dirty old work jacket that somebody had left aboard and the bottom half of a rain suit for pants. He didn't know beans about boats, and he sure didn't know about the slivers of steel cable that can lay a man's hand open like a knife. So I said to him, "Pardner, you're sure gonna need a pair of gloves for this work," and looking around, I spotted a pair of good leather ones lying on a stack of grass lines near the boiler deck steps. I noticed that the forefinger of one was a bit torn but didn't think anything of it. "Here, try these," I said and handed him the gloves.

Well, he put them on, then real quick pulled the left one off and gave it a shake. Something fell out. "God damn," said Earl, the other deckhand, with a tickled laugh, "why that there's Ol' John's finger."

Barf went the new man. Dead body parts or dead parts of a body don't go well with a hangover. Earl, he bent over and gave the finger a good look. "Neat job," he said, and started to kick it overboard.

"Hold on there, Earl," I said, "don't do that." Can you imagine just kicking a piece of a man overboard? Why, that finger came off so quick that there might be a mite of John's immortal soul trapped in it, and without a Christian sendoff, it and the balance of John might never meet again when the time came for him to go up or down yonder. The poor little tad of soul might spend an eternity wandering out there in the void looking to meet up again with John and never finding him.

"Why not?" asked Earl. "Tain't gonna do John no more good."

"I'm gonna take that back to the cook and get him to fix up a good mess of beans with it," I answered. This got a laugh from all the crew except for the new man, who was looking like maybe he'd call the whole thing a career right then and there.

Well, of course, you know I wasn't going to do any such thing. Shoot, there wasn't enough fat and juice in all of John's whole body for a good kettle of beans, much less in this little old piece of finger. I picked it up and looked it over. It was somewhat flattened and pale and by now a mite stiff, but it was for sure a finger, and that big gear had done a neat job. I stuffed it back into the left glove that the new man sure wasn't going to wear, wrapped the glove around a two-pound shackle pin, tied it all together with a long piece of cowtail, and walked over to the edge of the boat.

"I hereby consign this finger to the deep, and may the good Lord have mercy upon whatever mite of soul goes with it." With this I dropped it overboard, and there it lies to this day in three fathoms five at Mile 473.5.

I haven't seen Ol' John from that day to this, but John, wherever you are, pardner, rest assured that your finger got as dignified a burial as a man not in too good a state of grace could give it.

Thirty On, Thirty Off

I had set the clock for 4:30 A.M. Therefore, that was what time it must be, give or take ten minutes. My clock, a $3.00 Big Ben, was as lackadaisical about the passage of time as I was. Part of the reason I was a riverman was that I resent authority and regimentation, so on shore on my thirty days off, I let time go peter itself out wherever old hours go to die. When it was time to return to the boat and thirty days of work, the date and time became important again; they would determine when I must sleep and when I must work and when I must eat.

I glanced at my sleeping companion. She was curled into a fetal ball with the covers over her head. I had been with her since my wife and I called it a marriage. Making her happy pleased me. Throwing her out of my life had occurred to me. I would not wake her to say goodbye. I did not want her awake. Saying goodbye would be fuzzy-headed and stale-breathed, done more out of duty than need. I was returning to a world of men and boats and fog and weather.

She and I had a curious way of becoming cool, almost hostile, the last day or so before my departure. We would snipe and argue and stay apart. At first we worried about this, then a country-western ballad solved the mystery of our actions: "Make me hate you so I won't miss you when you're gone." We heard it at the same time, looked at each other, and laughed.

I got out of bed and walked to the window to check the weather. I was going to fly to Pittsburgh to catch my boat. The weather promised to be fair; the stars were bright and clear.

As I prepared to face a month in a world that I have always loved, I would begin a life of celibacy, masculine company, and occasional great nervous strain, but it was worth it. I felt sorry for ordinary men and their normal lives. I felt some of the river kind of life was good for me—I needed to escape the cloying life of constant warmth and safety, the constant companionship of women and children, and go a-viking. I needed to know the trickle of icy rain down my neck, the feel of the wind piercing my body, the feel of cold hands and cold feet; I needed to know the presence of danger, the blackness of night, and basic hard work. I needed the camaraderie to be found in a good crew and the knowledge that my efforts were important in getting a huge tow to its destination.

Few occupations remain that test a man's mettle like that of towboat work, be he captain or deckhand; few test his mettle alongside his fellows, or the strength of his nerves in a tight place. The river life will tell him a lot about himself and, inevitably, not all that he discovers will be good. He may think himself a pretty tough customer until he falls among some really tough men. He may think himself intelligent until he meets intelligent men who do not equate verbosity with brains. He may find that he is truly inept. He may find that he is a coward. He may discover that he doesn't measure up. And that which he discovers he must live with for the rest of his life.

I continued packing. My clothes were already in the suitcase: three pairs of pants, three shirts, two sweaters, and an old Navy watch cap without which I could not steer a boat, six pairs of socks, and six each top and bottom underwear. This was packing for pilothouse duty. Also into the suitcase I dumped two books that I wanted to read but might very well not, three magazines, which I would read, legal pad, envelopes, stamps, felt-tip pens, and a carton of cigarettes. I also included a pipe and tobacco, which, once again, I would try to learn to love and cherish while I gave up cigarettes. I was wasting my efforts, I knew. It would never work. The first time I had a difficult lock approach and could not lay my hands on a cigarette, the whole crew had better begin donning life jackets.

I put on my old navy pea coat and my extra hat. There was nothing more to do but wait for the taxi. The bundle in the bed never stirred, and I wandered quietly about the apartment. The way I took leave might make it seem I was departing for a three-year whaling voyage instead of a thirty-day stretch on the river, where I would never be out of sight of land except in a dense fog. But my home meant a great deal to me. I had simple needs, only slightly more than "three hots and a flop," as a friend of mine so succinctly put it. My apartment wasn't big or fancy, but it was all mine. (Perhaps I should say "ours," for I had hopes that the sleeping beauty would become a permanent resident. You know, like a wife.) The apartment was like the inside of my head, interesting but not very well organized. I have always had a powerful territorial instinct. I never needed much space, but I had to have a place where I could discard my armor, keep my rear well guarded, and roll in my own middens. I knew my home's smells, its contours by night, where not to put my shins and big toes, and where to place my hands day or night on whatever I needed. It was filled with books and plants and records and bad metal sculpture, mostly my own.

When I came back home again, I would nose around the rooms like an old dog, seeking reassurance that everything was still just as I left it. I preferred at those times that my ladyfriend not be there, for I wanted to remesh my senses with those mysterious forces that made this my home. I needed a few hours alone to get settled in.

Likewise, when I got to the boat, I would need several days to settle back into life on the water. It would take a couple of days, a half-dozen watches, before the body would adjust, before restful sleep would come and I would once again feel myself a sharp and proficient riverman.

I saw the taxi pull up. I returned to the bedroom and gazed for a moment at the unmoving bundle in the bed, gave her a light kiss on the bit of blonde head that showed, and waved her a silent goodbye. Before I left, I scribbled a note: "Be good! Have a good day! Will call from Pittsburgh to report the safe arrival of me. If I do not call right away, do not presume me dead and start converting my squirrel's hoard of material goods into what little cash it will bring. See ya! Love, Jim."

Then I departed, silently but not unhappily.

Ghosts on the River

I have found that most river people believe in ghosts. They tell of banshee wails and whispering voices coming over the tow head's speaker on foggy nights, strange faces appearing in the engine room.

Do I believe in ghosts? Of course.

Especially after a certain night piloting near Portsmouth. I was upbound about a half mile below the U.S. Grant bridge, pushing a tow of thirteen empty tank and coal barges. It was almost midnight. Fifteen more minutes and I would have been off watch. There was a shut-out fog, zilch visibility, and I had long since called for downbound traffic around New Boston approximately two miles upstream. I had received no answer, indicating that there was no one heading my way, or if there was, he had his radio off or turned way down. Both of which are major no-no's, especially in fog. I called again for traffic downbound around Fullerton Light, about three quarters of a mile above the bridge. Still no answer. So I felt safe in proceeding upriver.

The bridge itself was no real threat, even in fog, with its more than 600-foot horizontal clearance between piers. I was pretty much committed to shoving through the bridge safely and was looking forward to being relieved by the after-watch pilot and going to bed.

The tow was pretty much in the middle of the river, splitting the distance about equally between the two piers, and the head was just about a hundred yards from commitment under the span. I glanced at the radar, mostly from habit. Nothing alarming registered. I turned away again to stare out into the opaque void ahead. Of course, I could see nothing but swirling fog. Certainly not the head of our tow, which was 900 feet away. In fact, I could barely see the handrails around the pilothouse.

I glanced back quickly at the radar. This time something registered: a huge something where nothing should be. My watch cap just about jumped off of my head and my internal Klaxon sounded. Right in the middle of the screen and on a positive head-on collision course with my tow was a huge object, so close that evasion was impossible. I was about to face up on a downbound tow.

My first reaction was deep anger that this oncoming idiot would be moving downriver with his radio off, without ever calling for upbound traffic. I grabbed the transmitter, put the rudders hard over to starboard in an attempt to minimize the collision, and at the same time, I called him on the radio; I didn't bother with formalities but just screamed, "Cap, we're about to face up on each other. I got her hard down starboard. You better do the same to port. See you on the one if we're lucky." I got no answer.

My tow was now swinging violently to starboard. His stayed on straight rudder, with no attempt at evasion. I thought maybe his radar was out of commission as well as his mind. He kept right on coming.

Then we hit, we merged, we melded one into the other. But dead silence reigned. Where was the crash? My tow passed right through the port bow corner of his tow without so much as a bump. I had just passed through solid steel ectoplasm, the inland river version of the *Flying Dutchman*. I suddenly realized that his tow was not moving, only mine, and was it ever moving!

Soon the noise of a collision did come, not steel to steel but rather steel to concrete. It was the sound of my starboard side hitting the bridge pier. About then my other pilot was up in the wheelhouse saying, "Gawd almighty, who is that and what you all doing?" I didn't bother to explain. I still had to get the tow stopped before we slammed into the Kentucky bank.

We went from full ahead to full astern just as fast as I could haul back on the throttles. The boat bucked in her face wires and commenced jumping up and down. Between the drag on the pier and the backing of the boat's huge wheels, we got her stopped. All this activity kept me so busy that I momentarily forgot my recent adversary.

When I looked at the radar again, there was that other tow sitting dead still right in the same spot where he had recently scared a decade off my life. By now I was busy trying to get the tow back on course, the head pointed back out into the river without letting the boat hit the piers or drag its wheels and rudders over the rocky bank. I steered hard to port and safe, deep water. As we got back on course, the radar showed the stranger to be no more. There was not a trace of him up or down the river or even in the middle of the river where he had so recently been floating. This was getting "curiouser and curiouser." No radio contact, no radar image, just a great expanse of uninhabited river with a light yellowish sheen on the surface, as though a sinking vessel with all its lights still on had settled to its silted and murky final resting place.

We proceeded serenely up the river. The boat, that is, not me.

On my next trip around Portsmouth, I saw the boat again. And on several subsequent trips. After the first night I did not hit the panic button but just sailed right through the ghostly tow, always, however, with a certain trepidation that this time his steely ectoplasm might have jelled. I never failed to call for traffic, and he never answered.

In my late-night boredom I started to look forward to his short-lived ethereal appearances. Late-night watches make you a little strange sometimes, and any diversion, especially an unexplained mystery, takes a few minutes off the clock and brings you closer to going off watch and to bed.

I kept hoping that some dark night a long-sunken steamboat would rise slowly to the surface, dripping algae and river mud, its lights blazing, faint music playing, pale roustabouts on the main deck, fashionably bedecked ladies and gentlemen strolling about on the promenade deck taking the air. The boat would have a gaping hole in her bow or a missing side from whence her exploded boilers had taken flight. Sad to say, she never appeared to me. Maybe another pilot got the dubious honor. If so, he never told anyone. Confinement and Thorazine tend to quiet one down. And the home office takes a dim view of pilots who see things, tending as the office types do, to attribute hallucinations to controlled substances and other forbidden stimuli.

Then one night I met an old captain friend in a bright little bistro called the Buffalo Bar, a favored way station for those of us who like the peripatetic life. We were trying to out-story each other, as men who drink and go a-wandering are wont to do. He had been at riverboating longer than I had and had stored up more tall tales than I could ever match. Eight-foot catfish, sure thing!

I countered with my tale of the Portsmouth poltergeist. My friend looked bored, and I had the sinking feeling that he had heard it all before. Dash it all, old man, I thought, is there nothing under the sun or the water that you old geezers haven't lied about?

"Well, good captain, let me tell you about your ghost," he began.

"No, no," I silently cried. "I do not want it explained. I want to go to my grave believing in it. Why take all the flavor out of a poor boatman's life? I love a mystery as all of us do." I hadn't been up Portsmouth way for some time and was looking forward to the possibility that on my next trip I would finally see the doomed craft and her spectral occupants.

But the old motormouth was not to be denied. His advice: "Check your chart just above the bridge, and you will see in *very, very* tiny letters the word, 'Tower.' This tower is the Kentucky side support of a set of high-tension wires leading to Portsmouth. There are four wires and they are equipped, every few hundred feet or so, with big red balls. These are radar balls designed to give you a good solid blip on the scope, especially during high water when the line sag is closest to the river. The lines and balls are close enough to the bridge so that both obstacles sort of meld together and form one big image very much like an oncoming towboat. You probably noticed that as you began to clear the bridge that the ghost disappeared or you ran right over or through it. Lordy, the first time it happened to me it like to give me a heart attack!"

This know-it-all reduced my ghostly towboat or spectral steamboat to no more than a mundane, utilitarian power line and bridge that had confused the radar, which electronically warped their image into that of my oncoming towboat. Power-line images, he informed me, come in all shapes and sizes. They can resemble buoys, boats, driftwood, skinny bridges, and galaxy-like blobs. And with more experience, I did encounter some of these phenomena.

Of course, all this doesn't prove there *isn't* a sunken steamboat that rises at midnight to scare lonely pilots, or that I hadn't rammed an unsubstantial towboat that first night. I stand by what I told the crew. When they asked me at breakfast what the midnight excitement was all about, I just smiled foolishly and said, "I saw a ghost."

Who Could Ask for More?

The knock came, the door opened, and the deckhand said quietly, "Time, Cap." It was 5:30 A.M., and I had half an hour to dress, clean myself up, have breakfast, and get to the pilothouse. For the second or two that the door was open, I caught a glimpse of the world outside. It was clear and cold, dawn only minutes away. I felt really great, well-rested, and hungry. This was absolutely the best time of the day for man. I felt completely in control of my environment, from my relationship with my shipmates to my ability to handle the boat with skill.

Pancakes for breakfast! Perfect size, texture, and flavor. Why, oh why, couldn't wives and girlfriends cook like this? I can honestly say that in an adult lifetime spent as husband and lover, I never met a woman who could do pancakes. Compared to riverboat cooks, the culinary efforts of modern women are like those of blacksmiths. I ate breakfast hurriedly because I was eager to get to the pilothouse, get rid of the pilot and anybody else who was there, and welcome the dawn all alone.

I did not encourage the pilot to recount his night's adventures. I was interested and would find out later, but at the moment I wanted to be alone with my thoughts and my coffee and cigarettes to savor the beginning of this new day in my life.

We were at Mile 259, Hoggs Landing Light, downbound with empties for a refinery. According to the compass indicator on the chart, we were heading slightly south of due west, so the dawn was coming up like a polonaise out of Pittsburgh, now so far behind us. The moment was utterly entrancing; all things conspired to make this a glorious morning. The coffee was hot and good, the day's second cigarette was still tasty, not like the one a pack and a half later when your mouth feels like a pot-bellied stove.

There was not another boat in sight, nor a human nor a motor car, train, or plane. The river was like a millpond, and the world was silent except for the unnoticed noises of the boat. The world was mine, though I gladly shared it with the only other living creatures in evidence, the great hunched-shouldered turkey buzzards that perched in the still, stark, leafless trees, and only bestirred themselves when we passed and then only to the extent of rising effortlessly, majestically, into the air, and when we were gone, resettling like unnatural fruit back into the same trees.

The tow, as though sensing my control and well-being, was as docile as a baby. I could have done no wrong that morning even if I'd tried. The only dark cloud on the horizon was Gallipolis Lock, but that was hours off, and I did not clutter up my euphoric state with thoughts of future terror. It wouldn't be that bad in this stage of water, and if I and my brother pilots contemplated possible disasters, we would have to leave this profession.

As we were about a half a day from the refinery, I figured that we would be making a downbound run to Cincinnati the next trip, the prospect of which pleased me. It would break up the tour of duty. We hadn't been there in four or five trips, and it was an easy stretch of steering, which was good, because if I knew the dispatcher, they would overload us unmercifully. Also, at approximately thirty miles out of Cincinnati, which would be a good two days of pumping off, I would be able to receive my favorite radio station, WGUC, the University of Cincinnati FM station, and saturate myself with classical music and—praise the gods of good chance—perhaps the Saturday afternoon opera. There is no other place on the inland waterways I have been able to pick up the kind of programming that rivals this station.

Another good thing about going to Cincinnati was that it put me in reach of my ladyfriend, whom I already missed a great deal. She would come to the boat and ride a watch with me, or I would take several off-duty hours and she and I would have dinner together somewhere. Not at the apartment. The inevitable intimacy there would upset my new and delicate state of adjustment to celibacy, and I would have to start all over again. Leaving the boat was sometimes not worth doing, since it was only fair to permit others to leave if the captain did, and with some crews that could mean worrying about their condition when they returned—if they did. It always made me nervous to have any of the crew off the boat; we were then not a fully functioning vessel, and if anything should happen that required all hands or we suddenly received a change of orders and were expected to depart immediately, I would be a mighty embarrassed captain when I asked for extra time because my crew was scattered to the four winds. When lay time approached, I always breathed a silent prayer that the company would keep us busy enough to make shore leave out of the question—even if that meant forgoing it myself.

At the moment, there was no place in the world I would rather be than where I was. There was no one in the world I would rather be than me. I would not want to be at the controls of an airplane screaming through the sky, though I knew it must be beautiful up there on such a fine morning. Planes were too fast and too unnatural for a contemplative man like me. A train? Too noisy, dirty, brash, and unserene. A truck? Too commonplace.

Other pleasurable human activities, even sex, pale to insignificance when a man achieves a rare moment like the one I experienced that morning on the Ohio—a moment when he is totally at peace with himself and completely one with his surroundings. Alone he may be, but no matter. He questions not his competence, for what he is and what he does prove his possession of that quality, and for a short while he is unassailed by self-doubt. He is not competitive, for there is no competition in sight; even his deepest inner fears are granted surcease for this time.

I thought: "I am such a lucky man. Lucky because I feel content most of the time and not just during euphoric moments like this." I asked myself, "What more could I want?" and I answered, "Nothing." Grand foods? Food is merely fuel, and I already ate better than most of my fellow human beings. Women? Nonsense. One is enough for any man. Money? It wasn't my bag. Prestige? My work and the way I did it gave me that. Self-respect and the respect of others I already had. Dignity? I could have used a little less of the straightlaced brand. Lord knows I had dignified myself right out of the regard of some very willing ladies, only to fall afoul of the one I had then, who thought I had an overabundance of it and did not seem to mind, in fact, found it admirable. But it is better to have dignity than not, for there are moments in life when you are reduced to little more.

My work was interesting and challenging. It had made a believer out of me—a believer in me. My mind was insatiably curious, and there were thousands of books still unread. My health was good and all my material wants under control. What more could a reasonable man ask for? I thought a moment. Yes, there was one thing. I would like to be able to fill the pilothouse with great music. Dvorak's Ninth Symphony, *The New World*, I thought would be appropriate for this great new day, which, as each day does, heralded a great and always amazing new world. Here at Hoggs Light, however, all I would be able to get was *Everybody's Farm Hour.*

I walked out on the bridge and breathed deeply of the crystal clear air. It was cold as the dickens, but spring was in those lungfuls of early morning. The tow held steady in the middle of the river, her bow never wavering off Campaign Bend Light. A glance astern filled me with a quiet pride, for the greater part of the boat was behind and beneath me, and all that I could see of her spoke of professionalism and of her good luck in having a crew that cared. The wake was smooth, straight, and perfectly synchronized.

I thought of the words Herman Melville gave to Captain Ahab in *Moby-Dick*. Ahab uttered them while in a black mood, despairing of ever finding the great white whale, but I thought of them in an ebullient mood, for lifted from context they could be said with joy: "I leave a white and turbid wake: pale waters, paler cheeks, where'er I sail. The billows sidelong swell do 'whelm my track; let them. *But first I pass.*" I looked back, and indeed our turbulent track was gone. It had been "'whelmed" by the great water through which it was made, but not before we passed.

Unscrambled Yegg

"Hey down there, anybody home?" I called on the intercom to the galley.

"It all depends on what you want," came the voice of him I sought.

"I want you, pardner! Up here on the double if not a little faster!"

Despite the words, my voice did not communicate emergency.

"Yessir, Captain, sir! Right away, sir!"

Shortly, but certainly not in double time, I felt the faint vibration of the pilothouse as someone climbed the steps. The door opened and Glenn entered.

If there is such a thing as neighborhood nepotism, then I must admit to having practiced it on the river. Glenn lived near me in a little conservative, hilltop Bohemia in Cincinnati called Mt. Adams. At the time I had an apartment there, the hill was largely peopled—in addition to its oldtime German Dutch residents—by artists, shopkeepers, and a large sprinkling of flower children.

One day Glenn showed up in, or rather returned to, Mt. Adams, for he had lived there before. And he spread terror among those pollen-sniffing innocents, for he was returning from a sojourn of several years in California, and it was reported and certainly not refuted by him that he had ridden with the "Wild Bunch." He was returning to home port for post-trauma R&R after one of his jolly comrades had scrambled his brains with a piece of iron pipe. And he could indeed, back in those days, be a bad egg. For when his brains finally came to rest, they were arranged in a pattern of drinking and delight in and proneness to violence toward the flower children and, worse, toward policemen, an unwise behavior that could lead to further scrambling.

Glenn adopted the swastika as his personal emblem and rode a fine old Zundapp motorcycle with a flair that was the envy of all members of the fraternity of cyclists, including myself. In defiance of the law, he wore a leather World War I flying helmet complete with goggles; he smoked a long cigar and could often be seen riding even in the most perilous traffic—"Look, Ma, no hands." He started his own motorcycle club, complete with colors, called the Mt. Adams Goons, or some such name. The group would meet for cookouts and other skulduggery in his front yard, and everyone gave them a wide berth. Including me, at first.

But after a year or two Glenn began to gentle down and bathe regularly, and he and I became friendly, though I still never turned my back on him. He maintained his semimilitary motorcyclist mode of dress, but the fires of violence were fading from his eyes, and Mother Nature was busily at work between his ears setting to rights that sparsely furnished space.

Glenn had often professed a desire to work on the river, and the day came when I desperately needed a deckhand. I figured that Glenn was at least a known if still somewhat suspect quantity and thus better than what the home office might come up with. So I called him to catch the boat. He showed up at Ashland, Kentucky, and came aboard looking like the great god of all the Iron Horsemen east of the Mississippi River: tight dungarees, engineer boots, embroidered shirt, dungaree jacket bearing proudly the colors of his cycle club, and a ring in his ear.

"Good God," I thought, "what have I inflicted on the nation's inland waterways?" Then a more chilling thought struck: "What have I inflicted on myself and my poor boat and her crew?" I almost said, "Thanks but no thanks" then and there.

Everybody on the boat gave Glenn a lot of room. He was just big and threatening enough that they didn't dare put him through the usual hazing but took a "wait and see" attitude. He didn't know a thing about the river, never pretended that he did, and he set about learning his job with a zeal and aptitude that astounded me. He was polite, clean, and cheerful and had a great ability to tell stories on himself rather than about himself that were truly hilarious. He was soon accepted by everyone, and his skills continued to improve. He started to work on steering and aspired to being a pilot one day.

That's how Glenn happened to be the man on the other end of the intercom when I called for a deckhand on the double.

"Howdy! Howdy! Howdy! Captain Jim." As Glenn approached the pilothouse, each "howdy" was given a rising inflection. He extended his hand and we shook. I had just returned to the boat.

"Howdy yourself, Glenn. How ya been? Or more important, have you, in my absence, been earning that ridiculous sum of money we pay you each day for eating as much as any two men?"

"I sure have, and the cook is running out of everything." Glenn laughed and then asked, "Anything new happening on the Hill? Anybody miss me? Anybody ask about me?"

I knew who he meant, and she did both.

"Well, yes, as a matter of fact someone did," I replied. "The nice elderly lady who runs the bakery asked how you were, and said to tell you hello."

"Har! Har! Har! Come on, be serious, did you see her?" *Her*, of course, being his latest lady friend.

"Well, yes, I did. She did ask about you and she does miss you. She asked me to reassure you that this guy Tim she's seeing is no more than a diversion to lighten the days till you get back. 'A cheap affair of the flesh,' she called it, and said that you mustn't worry about it."

"Arrgh!" Glenn said.

"Oh, incidentally, I got another message for you. Brumfield says to tell you to stay out of town or he'll nail your hide to the front door of Crowley's Saloon. I don't want to upset you, but he did ask me to pass it on." I waited for an answer. I knew he was trying to decide whether to take me seriously.

Brumfield was a gnomelike, lugubrious humor columnist for one of the local papers. Despite his dour appearance, he could be very funny in a black sort of way. He was from Hopkinsville, Kentucky, and strictly took "nuthin' offen nobody." Hilltop legend had it that he punched Glenn in the mouth one night during the height of Glenn's warlike years and actually got away with it.

Glenn decided not to take me seriously, which was the right decision. In the first place, I doubt if the Brumfield punch ever happened, but Glenn knew the rumor existed. As for the recent threat, being a Hopkinsville boy, Brumfield would never announce his intentions in advance. High noon drama happens only in movies like *High Noon*. The "code of the hills" fails to state but strongly implies that from behind a tree and in the dark of the moon is the best and safest way to settle an affair of honor. "That little pipsqueak wouldn't dare come near Crowley's," Glenn said with mock bluster. "I'd sic my boys on him." Boys that he and I both knew he didn't have any more. Gentleness may please the Lord but doesn't cut it with the black leather bunch, and Glenn had decidedly gentled down. His comrades had long since forked their phallic broncs and drifted off to find a new war chief whose chrome-plated swastika still shone with undiminished luster.

Well, many years have passed since I last worked with Glenn on a boat. The last time I saw him he was still wearing the earring and the military gear. Since the look obviously wasn't designed to alienate his shipmates, I figured maybe it was effective in doing business with the ladies. If I had been convinced of that, I would have worn an earring myself, not only in each ear but in my nose as well. Of course, now every kid on the street looks like Glenn.

Or should I say "Captain Glenn"? It would be a pleasure to ride a boat with him once more.

Christmas on the River

I have probably spent more Christmases afloat than on dry land. Except when I was a boy living on steamboats and at the yacht club, I spent them away from my family on a variety of craft in a variety of places: on a ship in the Whangpoo River at Shanghai China, a ship in the Panama Canal, a ferry boat in Maine, a Norwegian freighter in New Orleans, a sailboat on Lake Erie, a houseboat on the Ohio River, a marina headboat (trying desperately to prevent it from taking an unauthorized trip down the river), and numerous tugboats and towboats.

On a towboat, where the crew is away from home for thirty days at a time, the men manage to pretend that Christmas is a matter of indifference to them. This is of course not true. Most would rather be with their families. The few days preceding Christmas are often as lonely as the holiday itself. In the evening as you pass the many lovely little river towns like Pomeroy, Gallipolis, Marietta, and Madison, you can see the Christmas trees and lights and busy shoppers and can sense the pleasant anticipation of all those folks on shore. The little red "Cold Beer" signs beckon, and you feel that you would give anything to be part of that happy throng. It is all a person can do to keep from tying off at the waterfront and jumping ship. And that has happened. It just becomes too much for some men.

Christmas mornings on the towboats we generally wished each other a Merry Christmas and griped a little about the cruel fate that separated us from loved ones, and that is about as far as our celebration went. There was seldom an exchange of presents, though over the years I have received several cartons of cigarettes and numerous bottles of aftershave. The most popular gift would have been bottles of cough medicine. When its alcoholic content was discovered, it accounted for more sudden "flu" epidemics on towboats, where booze is forbidden, than any Asian virus. The best gift we gave each other was a heightened camaraderie. We did for one day, this one special day, make an extra effort to be hearty and pleasant to our shipmates, and we donned clean work clothes. Slicker heads of hair and smoother jowls would not be seen on any other day of the year.

The holiday food was always special. On a boat that "feeds good," and most of them do, it is hard to imagine any improvement on daily fare. But on Christmas Day, the noon meal was something else: stick-to-the-ribs, gut-busting, down-home fare at its finest. It would include at least two meats, a fowl and a roast, plus three or four fresh vegetables, two kinds of salad, fresh fruit, pies, cake and ice cream, and a variety of drinks. It was all a person could do to stagger up to the pilothouse and stay awake during the next six hours of navigation.

It seemed to be a tradition also for towboats to "catch a willer," or tie off, wherever they might be, at about 11:00 A.M. on Christmas Day and not resume navigation until 1:00 P.M. This allowed the whole crew, both fore and aft watches, to eat together and share at least this one aspect of Christmas tradition. The crew on a boat is really a family (at least on a happy ship), but because of alternating watches we do not get to know the men on the opposite watch very well.

I have seen about half a dozen Christmas trees on towboats. Sometimes I would see colored lights around the galley windows, and there were always a few boats with banners bearing the usual holiday salutations. I remember one with a Santa Claus, sleigh, and reindeer affixed to the stacks on the boiler deck. These displays were usually on boats that had elderly women cooks. Often widowed and with grown children, the cooks tended to shift their motherly affections to the boat crew, and many tried to duplicate as much as possible their Christmas traditions and customs. Without them, Christmases afloat would indeed be dreary.

One Christmas on a boat I was running, we tied off a few miles above Meldahl Lock on the Ohio side. The river was very high and swift, and whole islands of driftwood were careening downstream. But we got a line out and settled in along the bank with no trouble. Our cook was a lovely lady named Virginia. Her Christmas meal was truly sumptuous, the galley had a small tree with lights and ornaments, and unbeknownst to us she had purchased an illicit pint of brandy on her last days off. Each crew member found a small paper cup in front of his dinner plate, and Virginia carefully divided that pint of brandy twelve ways. It was a fine and thoughtful gesture, and we all appreciated it. I would believe that what happened later was proof positive that booze and boating don't mix, but my share of the alcohol amounted to only about three-fourths of an ounce.

At 1:00 P.M., we turned loose and started upriver. We had twelve empty tank barges and were bound for the refinery at Ashland, Kentucky. Even in this river stage the trip ordinarily would take about thirty hours. Before we had been under way long, I had to make a crossover to get into slack water under a point. This required plowing through the drift, and as we did, a huge tree rolled out from under the tow and was swept under the boat. I immediately cut the power, but it was too late. The tree got into the propellers and rudders and sheared off a seven-foot-diameter, four-blade, stainless steel propeller. Shaft stub and wheel went to the bottom of the river. On half power, we barely made it to the refinery some seventy-eight hours later, and that was only with the help of another boat sent down to assist us.

Since the perils and demands of navigation do not stop for anything, Christmas is just another workday on the river. So most of us in the trade pretended that being out on the lonely water, and not with our families, was okay and just part of the job. But it was not a true feeling. On my boats the cook would often say a prayer at dinner, and the rough old river rats around the table would actually bow their heads and mumble "Amen." And if we happened to make a lock on Christmas Day, the lock's pay phone would have a long and anxious line of crew members waiting to touch home.

For no matter how positive and cheerful you try to make it, Christmas on towboats and cargo ships is a lonely time. And the one day of camaraderie cannot make up for the loneliness and longing, especially for children, whose holiday it is, after all. Even I, a fairly sensitive man, can only go through the usually bleak waterborne Christmases with, at best, playacting at good cheer, knowing full well that it is insincere. If you are lucky enough to get a turn at the phone it means more than all good food and short-term friendliness ever found by those who choose to spend their lives on rivers or the seas.

Hang It Up, Pappy—
Wherever You Are

One typical smoky gray afternoon, we were downbound on the Monongahela River with five big empty petroleum barges whose contents we had just discharged at Mile 24, Floreffe, Pennsylvania. We were approaching Glassport Bridge and bend, and I had radioed for upbound traffic. The big new *Steel Ranger* towboat with twelve loads of coal was coming up just below the bend, and we arranged for a one-whistle, port-to-port passing.

There was another boat downbound just ahead of me about several hundred yards, and I not only recognized her, having been captain on her for quite a while, but I also suspected that I knew who was piloting her. She was pushing just one monstrous empty cement barge, but it would have been difficult to see over even if you were standing on top of the pilothouse. Deciding to satisfy my curiosity, I called the boat on the radio, and sure enough, "Ol' Pappy" answered in his squeaky, countrified voice. He had been my pilot when I was on that boat and we were running the Kanawha River to Charleston, West Virginia.

Pappy was quite a feller. He was in his late sixties, a small feisty man (about five foot two) without an ounce of excess weight on his compact body. His hair was mostly gray. He wore glasses and always the same costume: plaid shirt, chino pants held up by suspenders, and bedroom slippers. He smoked, chewed tobacco, dipped snuff, and played the guitar, banjo, and harmonica. He was full of cleverness and quick wit, but he frightened the hell out of me in those small rivers and was about to do it again. Pappy, I'm sorry to say, was not what you might call a "natural pilot."

"How ya doin' this evening, Pappy?" I asked. I had assumed that the reason he didn't call traffic was because he'd heard my arrangements and would also take the one whistle. The upbound boat was not yet in sight and wouldn't be until the last moment.

"Doin' just fine, Captain," he replied. "How you like it up here on this little ol' river?"

"I can think of a lot of places I'd rather be," I answered with mock emphasis, "like back home for a start."

"Hee! Hee! Got that okay." I could just see him as he talked, holding the transmitter in one hand, the other stretching down to the steering lever he could barely reach and straining atop his milk crate platform to see where in the hell he was going and what was out front of that huge old barge. He was just starting to tell me about a new tool he'd invented out of old rope ends for the purpose of cleaning hair combs when he caught sight of the *Steel Ranger's* twelve big loads boiling up to the river right at him. Well, there came a sound out of that radio like he'd thrown the hand mike out the window and either his milk crate had slid out from under him or he'd followed the hand mike. Then he blew it. He was right in the middle of the river, but he was only one barge wide, and the upbound boat had already given way to Pappy's port side, so all Pappy had to do was steer to starboard and pass him on the one. No sweat. But not ol' Pappy. He threw her all astern and slewed around crosswise in the middle of the river, all 340 feet of him, and there he sat—me bearing down on him at about nine miles per hour and the *Steel Ranger* bearing up on him at about the same speed.

I was so surprised it took me a couple of seconds to clear my personal channels and get the messages running between my head and hands. I reckoned that the *Ranger's* pilot was having the same problem, for there was the same brief hesitation on his part. Then we both came to life and reacted with the command "All Stop!"—and then some. Neither of us had a prayer of getting around ol' Pappy. Wasn't much he could do either: being single screw, he didn't have much maneuverability. So there he sat right in my crosshairs and getting bigger all the time. Well, I hauled back on those two big engines without even bothering to stop at neutral, and if it had been possible to lay a patch in water, I'd sure have laid a dandy! When those big diesels and huge steel propellers finally got her stopped, you could have reached over the head of the tow and shaken Pappy's hand—or hit him a good lick upside the head, which, it struck me at the time, would have been more satisfying. If my barges had been loaded, he would have been pluckin' his banjo for the Good Lord right then, with a few of his mates listening in.

Meanwhile, down below, the *Ranger* was having a few problems too. Even with 5,000 horsepower, twelve full loads of coal aren't easy to stop. Those engines had to be just about jumping out of their beds, and you could see the coal piles quivering and jouncing with the need to keep going, while those two big ten-foot wheels were hollering stop! Finally they did, but you could have sure pitched a chunk of that coal through Pappy's side window, and if I'd been in the pilot's place, that's just what I would have done.

So, there we were: one tow below, one tow above, nerves a-jangle, and Pappy crosswise in between. Well, he must have sensed that he wasn't exactly in friendly company, so he sort of tiptoed out of there and on down the river without so much as a "thankee fellers." The *Ranger's* pilot and I sorted ourselves out and went our separate ways, but as we passed, we went out on our bridges and waved mightily to each other. A strong bond had grown between us in the last five minutes.

The next time I saw Pappy, and the last, was about half an hour later. He was stoogin' around at the Lock No. 2 arrival point, waiting his turn to lock. I called the lock to establish our place in line, and to my surprise—for Pappy was ahead of us—was told, "Come on down, Cap. She's all clear." Well, I told you that Pappy was feisty, and this was too much for him. He came on the air screeching, "What d'ya mean, come on down! I been waitin' here! God damn! Blah, blah, blah. I know my rights. Blah, blah, blah." But all to no avail.

As I sailed past him, I waved and said, "Tch, tch, Pappy. The FCC is everywhere." And that was probably the most satisfying radio transmission of my life. I still do not know why we got in first. It matters to me only that we did. Then to make things even more satisfying, just as we departed a big double upbound tow arrived. Pappy was going to have a good long wait.

I wonder if Pappy has hung it up or if he is still menacing other pilots. He is probably out there someplace—if the Good Lord or another boat hasn't got him by now.

Hoist by My Own Hippie

A nonfunctioning engine can cause a captain plenty of grief. But that is nothing compared to the machinations of deckhands trying to slide out of work. This I learned through more than one episode like the following.

We were about eight miles above Markland Lock on the Ohio, downbound. Now, a captain left alone and coffeeless in his pilothouse will always think up work for the crew. In truth there always *is* work to be done, but a lonely captain will come up with make-work if left too long to his own devices. On this particular night, Jerry and Henry, down in the galley, made the mistake of ignoring me for too long. I pressed the intercom; it wasn't a cup of coffee I needed but conversational diversion.

"Ahoy the galley," I sang out. "Ahoy" is not a riverman's term, but I sometimes used it. I have even said, "Thar she blows" to indicate a landmark, or "Belay that" when there was roughhousing. Literary snobbery it may have been, but I preferred such language to "Hey, you guys."

"Yeah, Cap," came the breathless voice of Henry, as though the body that supplied it had been busy as a church mouse. But he wasn't fooling me.

"What you fellers doin' down there?" I asked with sweet innocence.

"Nothin' much. I just now been checkin' the guard lights, Cap. Found two out on the port side. Ol' Jerry here's fixin' to sooge down the galley cabinets." Henry spoke with equally sweet innocence. He was an ex-hippie whom I had tried to convert into a more realistic way of life through many hours of conversation. He had just made a mistake. A judge will tell you, "Don't plead guilty. Come up with some kind of story." And a smart deckhand will tell you not to say, "Why nothin', Cap, what you got in mind?"

But ol' Henry couldn't outsmart me; he wasn't lazy enough. I mean, you have to be a really dedicated goldbrick to get away with goofing off. Now, I didn't doubt that Henry was telling the truth. He probably did take a stroll around to get some air, and changed two bulbs while he was at it, and it was also remotely possible that Jerry was at least studying some on those cabinets. But the men's stories would have to be better than that.

"You all sound like you been right busy," I said, baiting him just a mite. But he knew something was afoot. He knew the game was up. He and Jerry had let me sulk for too long.

"Sure have." Henry sounded real anxious to get back to work. I could almost see him mopping his brow.

"You need something up there?" It was like he was saying, "Shoot, Cap. I'm busy as all get out, but I'll sure drop it in a minute to take care of you, ol' buddy."

"Naw, Henry," I said, sorta closing the trap slow-like. "I don't need anything." I hesitated; Henry must have thought maybe he'd pulled it off. But no way. "However, I got a little job"—snap went the trap—"that

I'd kinda like to get started on. Come up to the pilothouse a second, will you?"

"Sure will."

I broke the connection, but the last few electronic molecules from below squeaked past the disconnect and unscrambled themselves in a balloon over the speaker as "Aw, shit."

The pilothouse door opened and closed, and a person—disembodied in the dark—said, "Hi, Cap." His tone was not particularly cheerful, but Henry was a good man, not given to sulking. I'd never had any trouble with him, but tonight he may have been engrossed in a good book or some great "think" that required that he be mostly left alone.

"Howdy, Henry," I said, real cheerful, because I was sitting in the catbird seat. Or so I thought—but I had flouted Clausewitz's first principle and underestimated my opponent. "You and Jerry feeling real ambitious tonight?" After rubbing it in like that, I deserved what I got.

"Well, if we don't," Henry said, "I've got a feeling we're about to."

I like that, a good sense of humor in a victim. I showed my appreciation with a small laugh. "Ha, ha," I chuckled, then continued. "The laundry room is about due for a going over. It needs painting, and I reckon it's been a long while since mortal eye has peered under the washer and dryer. You and Jerry pull 'em out, clean good, and start painting right there. Then push 'em back, wet paint won't hurt, and start on the overhead. Okay, Henry?" I concluded with an imperious cocking of the eye, which I forgot was wasted on him in the dark.

"Any particular color?" he asked. Did I feel a pulling on my leg? I wondered.

"Oh, just follow the old scheme. You know, dull red floor, battleship gray walls, and white overhead."

"Ain't got no red," he said. "The chief used the last gallon in the engine room."

"How are you fixed on black?"

"Got plenty of that."

"Well, paint 'er black."

"The whole thing?"

"No, just the floor."

"Oh," he said, then added, "lint'll sure show up easy on a black floor."

"Well, I reckon."

Henry studied some on that. The time until we would reach the lock was ticking away, and so was the bomb inside my head. "I guess we better let the floor go till last," he said.

"I reckon that'd be best, Henry, else you're likely to step in it while doing the walls and ceiling."

"That's sure true, but you still want us to do that patch under the washer and dryer first, huh?"

"I think so. Do that first, then the overhead, then the walls and shelves last. Seems that's most logical."

"Seems so. Course, we'll not get it all done tonight." This was in a questioning voice.

"I know, Henry. The other watch'll take over where you leave off." Dreading the thought of going through this routine again with Glenn, I was beginning to be sorry I ever stuck my big nose into the laundry room.

"Well," Henry said with a sigh, "I guess we better get at it." I did not answer. Whatever I said, he was bound to sit down and consider it a spell. He went to the door, but with a hand on the knob, he hesitated. "Say, Cap," he said like the small boy asking his father why he falls down every time he lifts both feet off the floor at the same time, "can I ask you something?"

"Why, sure, son." I almost added, "Here, come sit by my side. At a lower elevation to be sure . . ." Instead I asked, "What's on your mind?" failing entirely to hear the trap spring. Oh, Henry, you sly dog, you know me too well. When all else fails, appeal to the pedagogue that resides in all middle-aged men. Especially those in authority who have just exerted it on a young hippie. Now, I know that Henry and I sounded like a couple of yokels on the matter of the laundry room, but he was an intelligent man, and I always enjoyed talking to him. With the approach he took he could have brought up anything from aardvark to zoology, and I would have taken the bit in my teeth and run with it. So, tonight he chose abortion.

"Cap," he said, "my girlfriend might be pregnant." A small voice inside told me this was a bare-assed lie, but I told it to shut up. This boy was in trouble. He needed me. "She wants an abortion if she is, and I'm not sure but what I want her to go on and have it. The baby, that is, not the abortion. Do you think I got any rights in the matter?"

Well, it was strange that he should ask me that, because it just so happened that I did think he had rights. So, I was off to the races. The hell with the laundry room. I forgot all about it. The sound of my own voice was too intriguing. A laundry room can be painted any time, but a dissertation by me on a red hot issue was all important. Ol' Henry, he just sat there on his diabolical ass and pretended to listen. Once, so sure he was that I was thoroughly hooked, he excused himself and returned with a cup and helped himself to my coffee.

About the time I was catching my second wind, the radio interrupted and the lock man said, "Come on down."

"Be right there, pardner," I answered and quickly concluded my lecture. "So, you see, Henry, you do have rights. You have as much right to decide the fate of that baby as she does."

Henry got up and kinda stretched and yawned a mite, then said, "By golly, Cap, you're right." He started out the door to make ready for the lock, then paused again and added, "I just wish I knew for sure I was the father." Then he was gone.

And a little voice in me said, "You been had."

It was 10:20, and by the time we got through the lock it would be after 11:00 and time for routine watch-change and cleanup chores. "By God," I thought to myself, "that Henry's a whole lot lazier than I thought." And he hadn't even bothered to take his dirty coffee cup.

But Why, Man?

The towboat approached Wheeling, West Virginia, upbound, and as this old city came into view I could see the large island separating the two banks of the river: Wheeling Island. It belongs to the state of West Virginia, is about two miles long, and is occupied by both residences and businesses. Two bridges lead from the island into downtown Wheeling, one modern, the other an ornate historic suspension bridge. Under this bridge a man had just died.

I didn't know him but had come very close to being with him during his last moments of life. Why he chose to die, I don't know. Why he chose this utterly lonely and most unpleasant death is also a mystery. For me it was a beautiful night. For him it was the end of some kind of trail.

We were upbound, destination Pittsburgh. The river was up, the current swift, and I was steering the towboat *John K.* with a full load of petroleum barges into the teeth of a first-rate blizzard. The weather bothered me not at all. In fact, in the darkened pilothouse, with the silence of a heavy snowfall outside, my world seemed beautiful and even serene. Occasionally I would flip on one of the powerful eighteen-inch carbon arc searchlights and beam it straight ahead. I didn't need it for navigation; it was a purely aesthetic act, for I loved to watch the huge white flakes flow and seem to dance in the immensely bright, tight tunnel of light spearing out ahead of us. They were like great ornate dust motes in a beam of sunlight. As they flew headlong onto the hot lens of the light they seemed to be reacting to some fatal phototropic need.

It didn't occur to me on this night, while I gloried in being alive and healthy and happy and enraptured with beauty, that very nearby there was another who despaired, who saw no beauty, who did not welcome the morrow but knew only insoluble problems and viewed death as the only means of escape.

At 2:00 A.M. the radio, always quietly muttering and grumbling to itself, emitted a shriek, as though a knife were being turned in its innards, and then fell silent, its electronic complaints overridden by a transmitter opened nearby. Then a voice emerged, calm, detached, businesslike. It recited a string of call letters and numbers and then identified itself: "This is the West Virginia State Police calling the upbound boat clearing the Ninth Street Bridge. Come in please."

That could only be us; there were no other boats nearby. I had made it my business to know that long before I entered this narrow chute. We had this treacherous, close place to ourselves. So I knew that whatever had happened or was about to happen would one way or another include us. I had a foreboding: someone had died. That had to be it. There were no pleasure boats out this time of year, so it could not be one of them in distress. There were no barge fleets ahead, so it could not be runaways that must be rounded up. I thought for a moment of bank robbers making a getaway by water and the police asking me to put a powerful searchlight on them. "No, I will not," I rehearsed saying, "I do not want my pilothouse or me full of bullet holes," and then I immediately discarded this scene as fanciful and overly romantic. This had to be death. Suicide—people generally do not fall off bridges. It was the time of night for it, and it was the place.

I answered, "The *John K.* back. I reckon it's me you're calling, Skipper, go ahead."

"Captain, we have a report that a man jumped off the Ninth Street Bridge. I don't suppose you saw it happen or have seen anything of him?"

There was not even a note of hopefulness in the voice. He already knew, without knowing anything, that I hadn't. He knew the man was gone. His voice carried the weary, jaded tone of a man required to function at an unnatural hour, of a man who had seen too much of violent death. Well, I too had seen violent death but had seldom had to deal with it, and I was not beyond shock. Even at a death such as this. The death unseen, of a man unknown, seemed, without seeing the remains, to be a fictional occurrence. A death viewed—the mangled and swollen clay— is never fictional. It is sickening, humiliating, ego-shattering.

I have often wished that I could have answered the police in a kind of slow drawl, "Why, yes, Skipper, we have him aboard and none the worse for wear. He's having a cup of coffee in the galley and telling the boys, from what I can hear on the intercom, how glad he is to be alive." I wanted to shock that radio voice into some reaction over the death of a fellow human, burdened with trouble and so ill-equipped to deal with it that his only answer was to walk alone in the middle of the night, in the middle of a blizzard, to the middle of a bridge and hurl himself into the black, choppy, frigid waters below. And to do this with the lights of a modern city behind him. Couldn't those lights tell him that somewhere among them there might be help? Back there somewhere was a hand that could have grasped his hand before it fluttered so futilely to regain the rail in a last-second but second-too-late decision, born of terror and the instinct to live.

How often I have wished that my fancied transmission had been real and the suicidal man indeed aboard. I would have hugged that sodden man and hovered over him and filled him with hot coffee, food, and cigarettes, and provided light and enthusiasm and hopeful words. He would have been like an immortal to me, a man who had died but didn't die. A man with another chance, who had found out in those short terrible moments from steel to water that life, even so burdened, was ever so sweet.

I answered the voice on the radio, and I, too, sounded weary. "No sir, I haven't seen a thing. Visibility's pretty poor. Uh—how long ago did it happen?"

"Well, it must have been just a few minutes ago. A driver saw him jump and notified a police cruiser at the end of the bridge, and they called us. He must have just missed the stern of your boat."

Oh God, I thought, he might still be alive out there!

"I'm clearing with you, State Police," I said. "Get back to you later."

I punched the crew lounge button, and at the same time pulled the engines back and flipped on both searchlights. "One of you get up here on the double. Other head back to the stern. Man jumped off the bridge, may still be alive behind us."

The deckhand who raced into the pilothouse and I each manned a searchlight and swept the waters around the boat. The lights were partially ineffective because of back glare from the snow, but they served to light up a little of the dark choppy water. Occasionally I had to come slow ahead on the engines to maintain course, but I did not fear hurting the man with the propellers. If he were that close, the deckhand on the stern would see him. If he were already dead, I might be doing the next of kin a service: chopped up, he was not likely to be found; he'd not inflate himself with his own decay.

I would not risk one of our men in an open boat unless we found him. Our boats were oared, and in the stormy current a crewman could not possibly cover enough surface to be effective.

I'm glad the man who jumped from the bridge did not hit the boat, though his moments of terror and futile struggle would have been far less if he had, for surely he would have died almost instantly on the steel deck. If he had, I would not have heard his cries as he cartwheeled or plummeted in whatever attitude of flight he assumed in his downward rush to extinction. Nor would I have heard him hit because of the howl of the diesel exhausts. A thump might have penetrated my consciousness, but I would have attributed it to drift in the wheels. If he were broken but still alive, his anguished moans would have been in vain. He might have lain on the deck for hours before being discovered. If, on going off watch, I had found him broken and dying, I would have been repelled and not filled with love and encouragement. If his thread had been cut, and obviously it had, I was selfishly glad that he had chosen the water instead of the stern of the boat.

I remember wondering that night, fleetingly, irreverently, so much a man of my technological times, whether, as he fell and his body passed through the beam of the radar sweep and was bombarded by high intensity radio waves, if for one brief second he might have shown up as a blip on the radar screen. Whether I might have noticed and always wondered what that so-instantly-revealed and so-instantly-gone little shooting star–like blip of light had been. It's too bad that radars do not print out a record so that I might have gone back and satisfied my curiosity. "There," I could have said, "see that little black line? That is the electronic concept of death. That is a man, that little squiggle of ink is a man soon to be no more."

After half an hour of searching, we gave up. We were too big and unwieldy to maneuver in that close place among the many bridge piers, and our searchlights were not fully effective in the snow. The current had likely already swept the man we were searching for far behind us, even if the thirty- or forty-degree water hadn't yet done its work. I came full ahead on the engines, removed the radio hand set, and called the State Police. "I'm sure sorry, but there is no sign of your man," I said, "and I'm going to have to come ahead on this tow or drape it around a bridge pier."

He answered immediately, "Thank you, Captain, didn't figure you'd have any luck. They'll find him down around Lock 13, I 'spect. Well, thanks again. Good night." He cleared the frequency.

"Good night," I answered and did the same. We were under way once more. It was quiet now, except for the howl of the exhaust, which is such a constant noise that it seems noiseless, but the night was no longer serene. I played no more with the searchlights, found no more beauty in the snowfall. I walked to the boat's bridge and looked down at the black water and said aloud, "God damn you, River, you black, treacherous son of a bitch." I hated the river at that moment. It was so impersonal. It accepts its victims and begrudges them anything more than a ripple and a faint cry or two to mark the place of their passing. It doesn't hate or lust for life. It just accepts anyone who comes to it. It just rolls along and occasionally spews up whatever it does not absorb as sustenance, what it finds in its grasp, including the swollen, barely recognizable caricatures of what once were human beings. I didn't really hate the river; that is an irrational emotion. I just hated it for the balance of that night.

Educating Jerry

Pilothouse cleanup is a daily chore on a towboat, usually done around 8:00 or 9:00 A.M. On one particular morning when this chore fell to Jerry, my problem crew member, a young man's initiation into the world of real work began.

I couldn't get really angry with Jerry; there wasn't enough showing on which to hang such a feeling. He was one of those tractable, bovine men who perpetually wore an expression of mild and shocked surprise—never anger or outrage but faint hurt, as though someone had just jerked a lollipop out of his mouth.

When Jerry first came aboard, it was necessary to make him aware of the simplest rules of shipboard life: the need to get up on time, go to bed on time, bathe regularly, come to the table fully clothed—wearing shoes, socks, shirt, the works—his face washed, his hair combed, post-sleep phlegm expectorated, and the clinkers out of the corners of his eyes. He had, after much urging, made remarkable strides in these endeavors. Being pretty-looking to start with, he became an absolute joy to behold at meals, and he ate with an efficiency that I often wished he could apply to his work.

Jerry was young and strong but seemed to be interested in little beyond eating, sleeping, and watching television (he would literally watch even test patterns on TV). Though he usually would do what he was told, he worked without any enthusiasm or confidence. But I liked Jerry, and I was determined that when he left my boat, he would be a better man for the experience.

Could he be jarred into joining the human race? When the pilothouse floor had been swept and mopped and Jerry was about halfway through the chore of washing the windows, I decided that this was as good a time as any to start his education. I critically studied the windows he had done.

"Jerry," I said, "those windows look like shit!" He was startled, apparently not by the criticism but simply by the sudden realization that he was not alone and that whatever he was dreaming about had to be postponed. He stopped wearing a hole in the center of the pane he was working on and stood in place with the look of a man whose slice of bread, once again, had fallen butter side down.

"What's the matter with them?" he asked without a trace of resentment.

"Well, those are all square windows, Jerry, and they have corners. The corners have to be done too." The dirt on these windows was not dirt. It was twenty-four hours' worth of cigarette smoke.

"Here, let me show you," I said.

Jerry handed me the cleaner and the paper towels. I washed a pane. "See?"

He nodded.

I washed another pane, then another and another. I almost started whistling until I realized that I was being had. It wouldn't be the first time either. Outwitting deckhands is a full-time job.

"There, got the idea?" I thrust the materials back at him. "Just start from the beginning."

"Will do, Cap. You want me to do those you did over again?"

"No, they'll by okay, Jerry." I was quietly proud of those panes. I didn't want anybody messing them up.

He finished the windows.

"Anything else?" he asked.

I looked over the job. Not bad. He'd missed a lot of centers but the corners looked great. "What the hell," I thought, "tomorrow we'll work on the whole window concept." Aloud I said, "Yeah, now let's do the searchlight reflectors and front lenses while you've got the cleaner and towels."

"Okay. You want me to change the carbons while I'm at it?" This surprised me.

"No, the chief likes to do that himself." On some boats you couldn't get an engineer to touch anything with a wrench outside the engine room, but on this one the chief preferred to do such jobs. Still, Jerry's question accomplished several things. It conjured up a vision of him sheepishly reentering the pilothouse with the searchlight mechanism in his hand, saying, "Cap, look what just sorta fell off." But it also indicated that he just might know how to change a carbon. And if he did know how, at some time he must have taken an interest in learning something—and having learned, was volunteering to do it. This was really progress.

Jerry finished the reflectors and asked, "Anything else?"

"You do a good job?" I swiveled the lights around until they were pointing like two bug-eyed monsters straight into the pilothouse. At this range and at night, if suddenly flicked on, they would have an almost physical force. They looked good.

"Yep, sure did."

I could see that the carbons did need replacing. "Do you think you could change those carbons without stripping the set screws?"

"Sure can." Did I detect a spark of interest?

"Well, okay, then, go ahead and do it, but be careful. If you screw something up, the chief will get a big piece of both of our asses." Jerry grinned at this and assembled his tools and carbon sticks. These were always kept in the pilothouse. He performed the work with reasonable expertness and no parts left over.

"Where'd you learn that?" I asked.

"Watching the chief," he said. Then he blurted, "I'd like to work in the engine room.

"You would, huh? Well, we ain't got no openings in the engine room. And if you stay aboard, you're going to have to learn to be a deckhand first."

There was plenty of competition for towboat jobs, and no way would Jerry get to pick his own spot unless he could win the respect of his captain and shipmates and show some aptitude for engineer work.

His chance came to do that as we were about to lock a tow of twelve petroleum barges. We were upbound, approaching Meldahl Locks. Jerry and Henry, along with Gregg, the mate, were in the pilothouse all bundled up and "work vested" to talk over the lockage they would be making.

"Well, pardner," I said to Jerry, "tonight you're gonna work the tow head with Gregg." Jerry had never done this before but he was not overly worried as long as Gregg would be there to take care of him and do all the thinking. "Henry, you work the stern," I said. The stern was Jerry's usual station. "You all head on out. Gregg will be there soon, Jerry." Jerry's face fell. The deckhands departed.

"Gregg," I said with a wink, "I don't really care if you never make it out there." He knew what I was saying.

"I ain't in no hurry to get out there in the cold," he answered with a grin. "I'll wander out when Jerry's got it tied off and check his lines."

If Jerry passed our test and lived through it, he might make it as a riverman.

Jerry Locks Out

I reached over and switched on the tow speaker. I could see Henry and Jerry walking out onto the tow, Henry halting a few yards out and poor worried, dejected Jerry plodding on alone to the head to assume the job of conning this 1,000-foot tow into the lock. I was not going to let him get into any real trouble, but he didn't know that. For the first time in his life he was going to be required to do a responsible job. He was damn sure he didn't like it. He kept looking back over his shoulder to see if Gregg was on his way, and each look showed him the boat getting smaller while the tow, the oncoming lock wall, and all the great black space around and above him assumed more alarming proportions with each step.

The tow was on straight rudder, no slide, no winds, and the speed was good. We were in perfect shape. I could put her in that lock chamber with no one on the head at all, as could any competent pilot. These big locks were usually a piece of cake. But I was not going to let Jerry know that.

The lock was getting closer. I punched the tow-head speaker.

"On the air! Anybody out there?" This came out deliberately rather loud and harsh.

"Yeah, I'm here, Cap," a small voice answered.

"Well, speak up. I can't hear you."

"Cap, the speaker's too far away."

"For Christ's sake, then, move it over to you and talk loud and distinct." I wasn't gentle and reassuring. Jerry must be galvanized a little first. But soon my attitude would change, for the whole purpose of this maneuver was to help him. "Got your possum there handy?"

"I don't see it around here nowhere," he answered with slight panic. The boat and the tow were getting closer to the opening lock gates all the time. It would be Jerry's job to guide our twelve jumbo barges, each 195 feet long, into the lock, a huge bathtub-like concrete chamber that gave us a hundred feet to spare in length but just five feet in width. The possum was a rope bumper used by the deckhand to keep us from scraping the lock wall hard enough to create sparks.

"You better find it right quick and get back to the speaker, because I'm gonna need some information from you soon. Dip your possum in the river first and wet it down real good."

I flicked on both searchlights and aimed one at the gate opening and the other at the landward wall of the lock. With the entrance to the lock amply illuminated, all Jerry had to do was keep telling me the distance to the gate opening and bullnose as well as our distance off the long riverward wall.

"I got the possum, Cap, and she's real wetted down," Jerry called. His voice sounded more cheerful than when he started.

"Good for you, Jerry, but be careful you don't get that bumper

A tow about to enter the gates of a lock. The rounded tip of the riverward wall is the outer bullnose (courtesy of Corps of Engineers, Louisville, Kentucky).

pinched between the wall and the barge." He had just two and a half feet on either side of the barges, and the bumper could be jerked out of his hand and pulled into the water.

"Got that okay, Cap." Jerry hesitated a moment and asked, "Is Gregg on his way out? I sure don't see him."

"Not yet, Jerry, but don't worry, you're doing fine."

I realized then that I had not seen any small light flickering about where Jerry was working. He had forgotten his flashlight, and down where he was in the low water of the lock there would be confusing shadows and dark corners.

"I laid it down, Cap, and accidentally kicked it overboard." I knew that if I could see him up close he'd be wearing his butter-bread look again.

I began making demands on Jerry for information on our distance from the gate and the bullnose. I didn't want to make things seem too simple, for often they were not, and if a deckhand began to feel that his contributions to an operation were superfluous, he would begin to act superfluous. Next thing you knew, the deckhands would be dragging

Jerry's view from the head of the tow was similar to this one, with the captain and his own treasured bunk seeming miles away (courtesy of Corps of Engineers, Louisville, Kentucky).

sleeping bags out on the tow and playing the harmonica into the speaker while the pilot was busy ramming into lock walls.

I did not need a lot of the information I requested from the man on the head; my perceptions were often better than his because of the height of the pilothouse, but I wouldn't think of telling him so. Considerable exchange of information calmed the nerves, built confidence between me and the deckhand, and this modus operandi came in handy when things were not apple-pie easy. I kept the man out there informed on the position of the engines, engine changes, steering changes, and any predilections of the stern not to cooperate. He was expected to inform me of the distances off the walls, the angle of attack, speed, and any predilections of the tow to seek a violent union with the lock gates and chamber walls. Nothing infuriated me more than to have a deckhand lapse into long silences because he had decided that I didn't need information or to mumble through his tobacco chaw and a mouthful of spit or to speak in a whisper to preserve his larynx or on the assumption that I had bionic hearing. Hell, I didn't even have normal human hearing; years of welding inside barge hulls while people beat on the outside with sledgehammers had seen to that. The permanent ringing in my ears was louder than some of these guys talked.

"Okay," I said into the speaker, "where are we, Jerry?"

"Whatcha mean, Cap?" Panic lent a shrillness to Jerry's voice. A vision must have crossed his mind that I might not know where we were, and he sure as hell didn't, and there he was out there all alone. "Why, we're gettin' awful close to the lock. But I ain't sure which one."

"I know that, Jerry, and it don't matter which one, they're all pretty much the same; 'sides, you can ask the lockman the name of it when we get tied off. But I gotta have some facts here, like how far are we from the gates and like if we maintain course are we gonna miss the bullnose or rap it on the snout?" We were actually starting the lockgate approach now, so it was time to begin calming Jerry down. Gregg was down on the stern of the tow talking to Henry. He could get out to the head very quickly if we should need him, but just then the only two people in the world who missed him were his girlfriend and Jerry.

"Have we reached the gates yet?" I asked.

No answer. Jerry was thinking. Then it came to him, and he looked into the yawning vastness of the chamber illuminated by the searchlights. "Yeah, Cap, head of the tow is just passing them now."

"Okay, now you just keep giving me the distances as we pass the little white signs on the wall. They will tell you how far you are from the far gate of the chamber." This he did, and the numbers got smaller rapidly. The information would help me know when to slow down.

"Eight hundred feet, Cap."

"All right, Jerry, now I want you to get into the habit of glancing back along the tow once in a while and visualizing the angle of attack on the wall. If we stay as we are when we touch, what kinda shape we gonna be in?" We wanted to be as close to the wall as possible without rubbing it and bouncing. I could tell that if Jerry failed to have me work the head to the starboard away from the inner wall, then the port corner of the tow, where he was standing, was going to hit pretty hard. "What do you say?"

"She looks like she might hit a little, Cap," he answered. Then added, "Right where I'm at."

"Ain't no such thing as hitting a little, Jerry. I can see as well as you can that she's gonna hit. What do you want me to do about it?"

"Better steer her to the starboard a little," he said. Well, that instruction was nice and nautical.

"Steering to starboard," I said.

Silence from Jerry.

"Well?" I asked.

"Well, what?"

"How far are we from the wall now?"

"Oh, five feet, Cap."

"Five feet," I repeated. "Well, Jerry?"

"What, Cap?"

"How long you want this starboard steer? Pretty soon we'll be pointed at the starboard wall."

"Oh, yeah. Work the head to port a little bit. Looks pretty good now. Hold her on straight rudder." Business was picking up fast for Jerry now. He had three calculations to be constantly made, reported, then changed as we penetrated farther into the chamber.

"Well, what do you say? I need to be talked to back here. Keep it coming. How far off the starboard wall are we?" I asked.

"About five feet, Cap."

I let the head settle over to starboard.

"How far are we from the upper gate?"

"Whatcha mean, Cap?" Jerry was more nervous now. Too much happening too fast. Too much getting too big and too close too fast. Too many decisions being required of him.

"See anything of Gregg yet?" Jerry asked.

I did not answer his question.

"What I mean is, how far is that little four-foot-square piece of barge you're standing on from the upper gate? Look up, Jerry, the numbers on the wall will tell you."

"Three hundred, it says."

"Well, that is the distance you got to get this tow slowed down, stopped, and tied off."

I could see Jerry looking about for the floating mooring pin that rose in the lock wall with the water as the chamber slowly filled and the boat was taken to the next higher level.

"How far off the wall are we now?" I asked.

"'Bout two feet, Cap."

Time to ease her over on the wall, I decided.

"Jerry, you got your wet possum ready? That's gasoline you're ridin' on. Don't want no sparks."

"Sure have, Cap."

"How far to the gate?"

"One hundred feet, Cap."

"Now how far off the wall?"

"Still two feet, Cap." I knew this was wrong. We were closer than that. Closer than I wanted to be.

"How far to the gate now?"

"About eighty feet."

Jerry sounded tense. Of course, after he had done this maneuver more times it would sound like Twenty Questions.

"Ol' gate's getting big fast, ain't it?"

"Damn sure is. We're on the wall, Cap." This meant we were in good shape. We were moving a mite fast, but no problem. Of course, Jerry wasn't aware of how well we were doing. It all seemed scary as hell to him. It was lonely way out there on the head of the tow, with only a disembodied voice to talk to, one that sounded concerned only with what Jerry as the forward set of eyes could report and not with his well-being or comfort. A glance to the stern would show Jerry no reassuring glimpse of his floating home and its warmth and safety and lack of demands but only two glaring round eyes that moved restlessly around, searching, probing, like twin death rays, seeking him out; beyond that, there was only blackness. Ahead and around him was light and the soon-to-be enjoyed comfort of a tied-off tow contained in the huge bathtub of the lock chamber, but he still had to earn that peaceful situation. The sheer immensity of it all—the high forbidding walls, the huge tow, the distance away of the boat, the speed, the feeling of inability to do anything about any of these threatening things—guaranteed an insecure man like Jerry that he was sure as hell in the wrong place.

I pulled the engines back to idle ahead. We had plenty of speed for steering. Gregg was by now about halfway out on the tow and would be at the critical tie-off point by the time we arrived there. The starboard searchlight was now making a movie star of Jerry, and the port was dead set on the upper gate.

"Twenty-five feet from the pin . . . twenty feet . . . fifteen feet . . . on the wall." Jerry had seen Gregg coming and was beginning to sound like a real deckhand.

"Jerry, keep me posted on the distance off the wall and to the pin."

"Yeah, will do, Cap." Then silence.

"Well?"

"Oh," he said, as though asking: you mean now? "About ten inches off and twelve feet to the pin."

"Good, keep that coming. Let me know when we're eight or ten feet from the pin. Engines are backing slow. We'll stop her right at the pin. How's that for service?"

"Mighty fine, Cap." Jerry was full of spunk and self-confidence now that his ol' buddy Gregg was right there beside him. Better yet, he was alive and well and had made no big mistakes.

We were moving dead slow now as we approached the mooring pin to which Jerry must secure the line. Both engines were in idle, astern all rudders neutral. Jerry called out, "Ten feet to the pin, Cap." I applied a little more power astern. "Eight feet." More power, but she was almost stopped. "Five feet." A burst of full astern, then to neutral, and she floated dead in the water. Gregg and Jerry threw the lines out and secured us to the mooring pin.

We stayed moored in place until the giant bathtub filled and we were raised to the next pool of the river. We had no trouble clearing the hurdles on the way out of the lock. With Jerry's call "All clear the lower gate!" the job was done.

When Jerry came up to the pilothouse for his hero's cup of coffee, I asked, "That wasn't so bad, was it?"

"Naw, not too bad."

"You did good, Jerry."

"Gotcha, okay, Cap."

"In fact, you did so well I may let you handle Greenup Lock. We should be there on your watch if we make real good time."

"God damn!" Jerry said in mock anger.

I laughed and turned the speakers and searchlights off and put the throttles into the "company notch"—that is, full speed ahead.

Jerry had joined the ranks. He did get into the engine room eventually and became a pretty good engineer, keeping his equipment so clean and shiny it could be in a museum. So far as I know, Jerry is still out there on the river someplace, tending those great diesel engines.

The Luck of the Draw

Over the years I have lost a near-dozen friends on the Ohio and Mississippi. One was a wonderful man named Dick Carnes, who died trying to rescue his son. Both drowned. Another was a student of mine at Cincinnati's Inland Waterways Vocational School. On his first job as a deckhand he disappeared over the side of the towboat, with no witnesses. His body was never found.

A fall overboard or an accident is not always fatal. There have been some miraculous escapes. There was the man who lived through falling from a barge and being sucked under the tow—a supposed impossibility to survive. According to river lore, he popped up much bruised but alive and told his captain, "I done scraped and sanded your barge bottoms for you, but if you want 'em painted, you gotta do it yourself."

Who knows what events will work together to cause a happy or a sad outcome? The experiences of two men I knew come to mind.

Often when a tow is arranged and the wires placed and partly tightened up, a towboat will depart for its destination slowly, and the crew will do the final tightening and placing of running lights and speaker cords on the barges while under way. Leaving the Ashland Landing one night, I debated whether to do just that, but I didn't really think it was a safe practice, and decided to finish all the work before departing. Two men were out on the barges but with only one flashlight. Marty had forgotten his again.

Now, the pilot's view of a tow at night, in the areas not covered by searchlights, is a huge, vague, black mass with several moving bright spots from the crewmen's flashlights. The pilot must occasionally check these little moving lights to know what is going on out there. One of the hazards the men face is known as a "duckpond." This is a triangular patch of open water in the normally safe center of the tow, caused by the rounded corners on the bows of tank barges. Two curved bows side by side create a duckpond about six by twelve feet.

When everything was ready to go, I checked for southbound traffic above the Kenova, West Virginia, railroad bridge. We would be departing momentarily, and there was little for me to do at this point. My job would begin when I heard the cry "All gone." I checked once more on the men, and it occurred to me that there were no signs of life on the barges, but that only meant the men were finished with their work. There should be no problem. Still, I felt a small stirring of apprehension. Just to make sure everything was all right, I began playing the searchlight over the tow. I saw no one. I searched again, a little frantically, still no one. They should still have been out there or at least walking back to the boat.

Then on the periphery of the beam I detected movement. Not much, but definitely movement. I put the searchlight on it. It was a small white shape. I grabbed the binoculars. It was an apparently disembodied hand just barely extending above a timberhead.

I slammed out of the pilothouse, rushed down the steps, and ran without flashlight, heedless of obstacles. I arrived to discover that the hand belonged to John. He was lying on the deck with his other arm reaching as far as it would go into a duckpond. At the other end of it was the struggling form of Marty, trying to escape the lethal black water below but being pulled away from John's weakening grip.

Poor John was almost exhausted. He had been holding Marty by his life jacket collar for about eight minutes, against Marty's struggles and against a stiff current that was trying to sweep him under the high curved rake of the loaded barge. I threw myself down beside John and grabbed the other side of Marty's collar. Marty was no lightweight. It was all we could do to keep his head above water. We pulled and pulled, until I was about as exhausted as John, and finally we got Marty high enough out of the water so his elbows and forearms rested on the barge. Though he was near shock and almost blue with cold, he held on long enough for John and me to get a grip on his britches, and we hauled him out and upended him on the barge like a grounded grampus whale. About then the chief showed up, and the three of us stood around admiring our catch. But the catch was interested only in getting under a hot shower.

Of the many things that had worked to keep Marty out of the river's clutches, one of the most important was my decision to do all the barge tightening and tuning before leaving the harbor. If Marty had fallen as he did while the unfinished tow was moving, nothing could have saved him. He would have been instantly run over.

Another strange series of events happened during the construction of the Brent Spence Bridge at Cincinnati. The steel structures were prefabricated by a company in Pittsburgh and shipped downriver by barge. A competitor of my old harbor had landed the contract to supply the tugs and fleeting services for this company. My ex-deckhand Jerry Baker, "Little Bull"—he who nearly gave me a nervous breakdown when I tried to show off for my old pal Jack Meade—had been lured away from us by this other harbor. I had been truly sorry to lose Jerry. He hadn't repeated his dizzy performance of that night but continued to be the competent man I knew him to be.

On the bridge work, the harbor Jerry now worked for would sometimes meet the big long-haul towboats below the work site, at their fleet in Kentucky. They would take the barges out of tow and fleet them until they were called for by the superintendent of the erection job. Other times, and more dangerously for the tug crews, they would be required to meet the big boat above all the bridges, take the barges carrying bridge sections out of the tow, and move them down through the existing bridges themselves.

The tug company had sent an old, single-screw, single-rudder, high-profile antique to do this work. The boat required an engineer to shift the engine, hence there was a three-man crew: the pilot, the engineer, and Little Bull, the deckhand. Manual-shift engines were slow and awkward and often airlocked. But the boat was not a leaker or a fire trap and had plenty of power to handle two loads of bridge parts with no trouble.

On this occasion the river was up and very swift, and work on the bridge had come to a temporary halt, but barges of steel continued to arrive and be fleeted until needed. The tug met the long-haul boat above the bridges, got its two barges, and headed downstream to their fleet where the barges would wait until called for at the bridge site. The fleet where they were supposed to await their turn was located just below the Southern Railroad Bridge's Kentucky pier. The tug was handling the two barges with no problem, until it was about 150 yards above the Southern bridge. The pilot was favoring the Kentucky side. Then the single rudder simply dropped out of the boat!

No one knows how. It just happened, and with a single-screw boat the pilot had no way of maneuvering the tug and tow. His only hope of avoiding the bridge pier was to back and try to slow or stop. But it was no good; the current was too swift, and the whole tug got caught sideways in the current and was swept down on the pier. There was nothing the pilot could do but ride it out and broadcast disaster calls to all available tugs in the area, hoping that after hitting the pier he might bounce off and be swept on into clear water, where help was on its way. We sent one of our tugs to help out.

The barges hit the pier, broke the face wires, and escaped further damage. Not so the boat, which had hit the pier broadside and hung there for a few fearful moments before rolling over on its side. The pilot and the engineer scrambled down the side of the boat to the now exposed port side of the hull. They could see the rescue tug coming, and it got there just in time to take the two men off the hull.

No one knew where Little Bull was. The galley? The head? The engine room?

Just as the pilot and engineer got to safety, the boat rolled over and was tumbled upside down; it was several hundred yards down the river before it came to rest on the bottom. Because of the high water, several weeks went by before the hulk could be located, and divers were sent down to try to recover Little Bull's body. But the current was still too swift for them to work safely, and they were unsuccessful.

Little Bull stayed wherever he was until river conditions permitted another attempt at recovery. About three months after the accident, John Beattey, the best-known salvage man on the inland waterways, got to the site with his salvage rig and hoisted up the boat and its victim. We mourned our old friend's loss for a long time.

Days

After more than fifteen years of seeing the river from high above the water, first in a harbor tug, then from the pilothouse of a towboat, I began to dream of seeing it at its own level, at eighteen inches from the surface instead of thirty-five feet. I wanted to be part of the river. As the 1960s wore on, I kept wondering what it would be like to take a small boat along the length of the Ohio, then all the way to New Orleans, with just myself as captain and crew.

One day, downbound with a couple of empties for the Ashland Oil fleet and due to get off the boat for my "days," I saw my relief, Captain Bill, waiting on the wall at Lock No. 2 on the Monongahela. He soon popped into the pilothouse, coffee in hand and a smile on his face.

"Howdy, Cap," he said, "how ya doin'?"

"Just fine, Bill. No problems. We, or I should say you, are heading for Ashland, gathering up empties on the way. Then a loaded downbound trip to Cincinnati, Louisville, Owensboro, and Mt. Vernon, a nice trip that should use up a good piece of days."

"Sounds good to me," he said, and we talked business for a few minutes more, and then I said, "Bill, I got a favor to ask you."

"Well, let's hear it, Cap. I'm all ears." He wasn't kidding; Bill had ears as big as pork chops. But then he was big all over, especially in the middle. Too many ass-sittin' watches and too much good food. He was a fine partner, and we got along very well.

"I have a little twelve-foot aluminum skiff with a four horsepower outboard and a hankerin' to trailer her to Pittsburgh and then take her all the way to New Orleans. I figure it to take me about twenty-five to thirty days to make the trip, but it could run a little over that. So I'd like to take thirty-five days off this time and pay you back thirty-five days when I relieve you." I held my breath. I really wanted to make this trip and experience the whole river close up, and I also wanted to visit the many small river towns that so many of my compatriots hailed from and that I had glimpsed only in passing. But most important, though I am not an overly complex or introspective person, I wanted the solitude this trip would provide. It was the same syndrome that had once prompted me to see much of the country on a motorcycle. But motorcycles are too fast and infinitely more dangerous than small boats, even on big rivers.

Without hesitation, Bill said, "No problem, Cap. As far as I'm concerned its a deal and glad to do it. I 'spect you're the one who's gonna have the problems!"

"Well, I sure hope not and thanks a lot, Bill. Now I reckon I better get off this old lady 'cause the lower gates are starting to open."

"See you, Cap, and have a good trip," he said, and then turned his attention to the business at hand.

Back in Cincinnati I began to make my preparations to depart. I arranged for my lady friend of the time to ride to Pittsburgh with me, then bring the car and trailer back home. The little boat was named the *Mary Cecilia* (she was later named the *Kate* and then the *Nancy*—but that's another trio of stories! Suffice to say the women in question were less cooperative and benign than the boat and river).

The *Mary Cecilia* was an ordinary twelve-foot skiff, flat-bottomed and scow-bowed. She was light and stable and even with only four horsepower would make ten or twelve miles per hour. I had decked over the front half of the boat into which I put a large hatch for access to supplies, food, extra clothing, bedding, camera, books, writing materials, and a nine-shot .22 caliber revolver. Guns don't attract me as a rule—my fa-

The *Mary Cecilia* being readied for the long trip to New Orleans

Fish decoration on the *Mary Cecilia's* bow. I made it myself.

Here I am aboard the *Mary Cecilia*.

ther always said too many people were killed by "unloaded" guns—but a person would be a fool to go all the way down the river and camp on lonely banks totally unarmed. I made a fold-down seat in the deck which, when opened, allowed me to sit on the midships seat and row the boat—which I was to do many times, for exercise and to save gas.

My dog Dia and I had made many 50- to 100-mile trips with this boat, and I had full confidence that a trip of almost 2,000 miles would present few problems other than those of time and distance. There were certainly plenty of places, especially on the Ohio, to replenish gas and supplies. The Mississippi, of course, required more detailed advance planning, for there were fewer shoreside towns or yacht clubs on that river. The longest run without any stops available would be from Cairo, Illinois, to Carruthersville, Missouri, a distance of almost 140 miles. But I was aware of these hurdles and planned to pick up an extra five-gallon can of gas at Cairo. As it turned out, I still almost didn't make it.

My friend Mary and I arrived in Pittsburgh on a glorious, bright June afternoon. We went up the Allegheny River about five miles, where there was a convenient launching ramp, and put the boat into the water. As I prepared to shove off, there were tears and hugs and promises of eternal fealty, for Mary and I were in love and would miss each other sorely. The only advantage was the fact that these farewells were not new, because of my job. Still, saying goodbye in a place so far from home seemed to lend an added poignancy.

One last hug and I jumped into the boat and shoved off, headed down the Allegheny to the Ohio. I soon reached it; the river was in pool, gentle and welcoming. The sun was turning the water bright as hot barge steel, and as the boat reached its full speed, I almost forgot about the girl I left behind. Soon I would begin to miss her, and she would return to my thoughts many times before we were together again. But as I smelled the funky mix of oil and river water, passed the industrial outskirts of the city, and began to enjoy the willows and thick shrubs overhanging the river, I looked downstream only, to what might be ahead of me. I was exhilarated, and all I could think of was the adventure to come.

Time Out
1967

Happy Landings?

As I moseyed downriver, I stopped at Wheeling and some of the smaller towns for a short look around at the breeding grounds of professional rivermen: places like Crown City, Vanceburg, Rome, Ripley, and—probably the most prolific breeder of the breed—Manchester, Ohio. This nursery of inland seafarers produced Chick Lucas, the Lancasters, the Walkers, the Drydens, Little Bull, and lots of others.

Most of these small riparian burgs were of a piece. There was a main street, a highway passing through, a picture show (usually boarded up), some small neat houses surrounded by garden patches, cars up on blocks, a gas station or two, and an old-fashioned store that sold everything from food to ammunition. The main activity at this summer time of year among the oldsters seemed to be "jest a sittin', jawin', and countin' the cars" that passed through on their way to somewhere else. The youngsters among the men were off on towboats, in the service, farming, or working in some factory in the area. The leisure-time activities were procreating, fighting, and drinking, though many of the towns were dry and the folks were churchgoing people.

I would like to have stopped at Vevay and Jeffersonville, Indiana, and Louisville, Kentucky, but my timetable did not permit. So my first memorable stop after Cincinnati was Tell City, Indiana. I pulled into the boat dock there for gas and supplies and an overnight stay. Naturally everybody was curious about who I was, where I was from, where I was going, and why I was making "such a long trip in that little tin boat." When they found out my name was Coomer, they exclaimed, "Why shoot, they's Coomers here in Tell City."

Coomer is not a real common name, but my father's brothers, Stafford and Joe, had both lived in Tell City, and both had been rivermen before Staff got into the motel business and Joe died. A son of Joe's came down to the marina, asked me the usual questions, and said, "How's Uncle Harve?" (Harvey is my father's middle name, and also mine, though I seldom reveal that fact lest I get called "Jim Harve." When I once visited Burnside, Kentucky, where my father hails from, he was called Jim Harve and I was Jim Harve Jr., a cousin was called Billy Bob, another Jim Ed, and another Joe Don. I can't remember now the Tell City cousin's name, but I'm sure he had two of them.) I assured my long-lost relative that Pappy was fine, mean as ever, and had abandoned the river.

Young Tell City Coomer was about twenty-five years old, married, the father of four, and a truck driver for a lumber mill. Like all male Coomers except me, he was big and ornery-looking. It turned out he could drink like he had a hollow leg, something my father never did. We had a fine old time that night, talking. He had been born and raised in Tell City, he said, and had no hankering for the river life. He liked to be home at night. Or at least close to it.

Early next morning, bleary-eyed and tired, I shoved off. Next stop, Evansville, Indiana. There again, I pulled into a marina. After the usual inquisition, the boaters told me of a great marina party that had been held all the night before, and from the appearance of the survivors it had continued well into the day. Most looked and acted as if they wished they "was dead." One sprightly, rotund gentleman was still at it and between libations was picking over the carcass of a spitted and roasted sheep that had been invited to the party. Well, that was all right with me, and I ate a few well-done parts myself, then the gentleman offered me one of the creature's eyeballs that had fallen into the ashes. He even washed it off with a little rum. I turned it down, so he shrugged his shoulders and popped it into his mouth. It must have been pretty tough, for he chewed on it for some little time. That was too much for me. I filled my gas cans, hoisted aboard a six-pack, bid my friend and the near corpses farewell, and proceeded downriver past Evansville.

At Evansville Bend I camped out on a likely piece of beach with plenty of driftwood for a fire. I was damned glad to be away from savages who eat animals' eyeballs or any other similar parts. I arose early the next morning, loaded up, and took off. About half a minute after departure, in the middle of the river while making a crossover and staring an oncoming upbound tow square in its ugly face, my engine quit on me. Frantically, I manned the oars and commenced to row, hell-bent for the bank, with the towboat pilot blasting out on his huge Kahlenborg air horns the time-honored notes that mean "Get the fuck out of the way!"

"Shit, man," I yelled, "I'm doing the best I can!" And, though a near thing, the best I could do was good enough by about thirty feet. I hadn't done a foolish thing by crossing in front of him, I thought, for I had had plenty of time to get past him if the little mechanical jewel hadn't died on me.

I reached the Indiana bank at the Plaza Yacht Club and called the local outboard sales and service shop and talked with a mechanic. He listened to the boat's symptoms and considered them a moment, then said, "Son, did you open the vent on the gas tank after filling it?" The old light bulb came on over my head, and I answered, "Sure didn't." I didn't need for him to tell me what was wrong. A closed vent equals no air, which equals a vacuum, which equals no gas, just when you need it the most. I knew better but had been too busy sittin' and jawin' and eatin' weird stuff.

I continued on my way. At 7:30 P.M. I locked down at Lock 48. It was coming on dusk, a great time for peace, tranquility, and food. I found a lovely sand beach under Tobacco Patch Light, no longer on the charts, at Mile 815.6, and went ashore to make camp. Before long, a flat-bottomed fishing boat passed, headed upriver. After about two hundred yards it made a wide turn, came back to Tobacco Patch Light, and nosed ashore alongside my craft. The boat, a rickety looking, wide-beamed vessel of some seventeen feet, was powered by the most ancient-looking Evinrude I ever saw, and it was manned by two guys dressed in bib overalls. Now, a man all alone on the riverbank doesn't welcome total strangers who make a beeline for his campsite. I mentally located my trench shovel, hatchet, and pistol.

"Howdy," they said.

"Hi."

"What you doing?"

"Fixing to eat."

"Travel fer?"

"Pittsburgh."

"Where you going?"

"New Orleans."

"That's a fer piece. Reckon you better be careful on the lower. She's runnin' pretty good."

"Reckon I will."

"Mind if we come ashore?"

At this evidence of good manners I felt less edgy and decided that my life was in no immediate danger. The men were named Syl and Obie. If they had last names, they didn't volunteer them. They had met, they told me, about seven years earlier in a wild brawl at a riverfront saloon in Cairo, during the course of which one man and a lady of easy virtue had had their little everyday problems solved on a permanent basis. Syl and Obie had been friends ever since.

Syl was the older and could have been anywhere from forty-five to seventy; his nose had been broken and badly bent out of shape. His wife, he said, had died of the "cold robies" about a year before that brawl. Of the two, he was by far the more talkative. Obie was a battle-scarred man of some thirty-five years. He had a glass eye, acquired after a fishing accident when he was still a boy, and the rudiments of a second index finger on his left hand. Obie spent the evening squatted on his haunches, occasionally confirming but never disputing anything Syl said. He rolled Bugler cigarettes with amazing dexterity. Obie's wife had run off with an itinerant pipeline welder from East Texas.

It came out that the affection between the two men had had more than a little to do with the Cairo bloodbath, although neither Syl nor Obie had been charged with inflicting permanent damage on anyone. Syl managed to convey his feeling that after a long string of personal misfortunes that night of violence in Cairo had been a sort of (not his words) psychological catharsis for both men. They had pooled their meager resources and teamed up. They acquired an abandoned school bus and parked it on the riverbank for a home. They sold fish and cordwood to satisfy their modest cash needs. They made raisin jack, of which a gallon was resting in their boat. For their own use only, they insisted.

Syl and Obie had reduced life to its simplest and were if not exactly happy at least content. They had made their compromises and had grown gentle and introspective in the process. In their own way, they demonstrated that Homo sapiens, when spared the tensions and the wants and needs of modern life, was not a bad sort of animal after all.

We three had a pleasant evening together. The raisin jack was harsh and potent, and I took to chattering like a magpie. At about 11:00 P.M., without any vows to meet again, we said goodnight.

It was enough that three men met, were able to bridge a cultural gap, and parted company, all the richer for the experience.

In the End Is the Beginning

At 8:00 A.M. I departed Tobacco Patch Light. The sun was shining, the river smooth, and the current swift. The engine ran like a fine watch, and my breakfast of corned beef hash, fruit cocktail, and coffee rested comfortably on my stomach. The cloud formations were magnificent. I saw them as vast, billowy monuments to the grandeur of nature. How you see things certainly depends on circumstances. Had I suddenly been transported home and made responsible for a harbor or a towboat, those same clouds—such a delight to my eye and a stimulus to my imagination—would have been harbingers of rain and wind and would be a threat to my little flock of boats or barges.

That evening, around six, I arrived at Paducah Marine Ways in Paducah, Kentucky, Mile 934.2. I requested and got permission to moor in the protected waters between a dock barge and the shore.

Such a sweet berth was not to be had the next night. I got to Cairo Waterfront Service dock at 5:00 P.M. This was the last stop on the Ohio, so I decided to quit for the day and tackle the Lower Miss fresh in the morning. The dock had a two-boat landing, and the gentleman in charge was afraid my little boat would be damaged and that I would sue him, and he was afraid that his insurance company wouldn't cover the loss, and he was afraid his boss wouldn't like it. I left to seek shelter elsewhere.

No sooner had I pulled away than I saw two empty hopper barges moored bow to stern at the lower end of his harbor, parallel to the bank, their rake ends butted together. This gave me a perfect tunnel into protected water; I took it with great stealth and moored inside. Congratulating myself for outwitting a minor functionary, I ate dinner and went to sleep.

I slept soundly, so soundly I didn't hear the twenty-barge tow come in during the night. In the morning as I headed back out through the culvert originally formed by the two barges' rake ends, I found no open river. Just a rusting, scaling slab of steel blocking my exit. I had to take hat in hand and hie back to the landing office, twisting my forelock, and humbly beg the functionary to shift twenty barges to let me out.

To his everlasting credit, the man smiled and said, "Sort of outsmarted yourself, didn't you?" He had known I was there all night and didn't mind. He just didn't want the responsibility for my presence. He dispatched a tug to swing the twenty-barge tow enough for me to get out.

By seven-thirty I was under way again. A mile below lay the Mississippi. There was no question about the exact moment I left the Ohio and entered the bigger river. The demarcation line was definite: the demure, blue-green Ohio was overwhelmed by the muddy, roiling current of the Mississippi.

She was awesome, near flood stage, and full of drift. I am not fainthearted, but no man could claim he felt no trepidation or second thoughts about going down the Mississippi. There was just me and my little twelve-foot boat and the great, huge river that was so swift and wide it looked crowned in the middle, as if the country couldn't contain it.

A Crusoe Adventure

Robert Louis Stevenson once said, "The world is so full of a number of things that I think we should all be as happy as kings." He did not mean that we deserved to dine on kingly fare like peacock tongue and caviar or sleep in silken beds. He meant that to be happy living as freeborn commoners, we have only to use our imaginations, to observe, explore, and appreciate the world, and to enjoy the simple pleasures.

I had the opportunity to test Stevenson's idea during my small-boat journey to New Orleans. I had traveled all one day, covering eighty-one miles in the semitropical middle reaches of the Mississippi River. It was hot and cloudless, and relentless horseflies had followed me all afternoon, attracted by the salty sweat on my body. They became so bad at one point that I was forced to abandon ship, stay under water as much as possible, and push the boat along, to escape their painful bites.

Toward evening I spied a small island, of which there are many in this stretch of the river. The bigger ones have names; the smaller ones, merely numbers. This one was about a quarter of a mile long, and perhaps thirty to fifty yards wide. There was a small inlet in the shoreline, a sort of natural bay with a white sand beach. Indeed the whole island appeared to be sand, and its highest point, not counting the tree tops, was only about fifteen feet above the water's surface. On each arm of the bay the cottonwoods grew right down to the water's edge. It looked like a perfect, snug little harbor, a good place to spend the night. There was no air moving, no breeze except for the slight zephyr I created as I motored toward land. I beached the boat in the bay, shut down the engine, and total silence reigned in the world. The many birds I had observed from afar had flown away or become mute with alarm at my arrival. The mighty river, still swift, swept by without a murmur. A huge dragonfly hovered nearby but made no sound and displayed no lust for my blood, unlike the large, aggressive horseflies that had followed me all day. Aside from that beautiful winged hunter, the only other signs of life were three turtles sunning themselves on a half-submerged log well down the beach—and it is hard to detect life in a torpid turtle.

I got out of the boat and gazed at the world about me, beyond the limits of the island, and felt I could be the last man on earth. There were no signs of my fellow creatures or their works to be seen. Not a single towboat in sight, no houses, no towns on the far shore. No planes overhead, not even a church steeple on the distant shore to suggest the existence of higher ground and people. My footprint in the sand appeared to be the first and only sign of a human being on this beach. And so I dubbed this small island "Avalon."

As I rested and surveyed my surroundings, the birds, so lately alarmed, were starting to settle back into the trees and chatter among themselves. The dragonfly hovered like a helicopter. The turtles had not moved. The three species represented here, avian, insect, and reptilian, only heightened my feeling of timelessness. Their presence turned back the time clock of evolution, for though they survive in a somewhat altered form, they date back to an era before the concept of Homo sapiens occurred to who- or whatever is responsible for life on this lush but minor ball in space.

I imagined that the birds were exchanging warnings about this brash new phenomenon that had so rudely and suddenly entered their domain and boded bad times ahead. For didn't creatures like me kill creatures like them and the quiet gentle turtles for no good reason? Acute wariness must be the rule of the day.

I pitched my tent for later use, for, hot as it was, it would not be wise to sleep exposed in these climes. The little vampires of the night are particularly voracious in this part of the river. I gathered driftwood for the fire, brought the ice chest ashore, and was soon prepared to settle in. A short exploration of my island, a swim, a cold beer, then dinner were next in order.

As I walked toward the water to cool off, just above the surface I could see the small heads of deer, swimming toward the island. On the chance that some had already arrived, I approached the south end of the isle, where they seemed to be headed. I moved with extreme caution and, sure enough, found two deer taking their ease on the warm sand. Soon seven or eight had gathered. They had swum over to the island for the same reason I had stopped here, to cool off and rest. They were beautiful, dainty creatures with big sloe eyes and hooves so small that I wondered how they could swim so well. I had seen them in the Ohio many times, young deer barely grown out of their fawn spots as well as motherly does and antlered bucks. Once I almost parked a tow on Blennerhassett Island because of a blip I saw on the radar. I picked out the cause of it with a searchlight. It was the antlered head of a huge buck swimming for the mainland. He was right in front of my tow and wasn't going to make it without a major course correction on my part. So I made that correction, passed his ass on the one-whistle side, and plowed a goodly furrow in the mud of lower Blennerhassett.

I left these deer to their rest and proceeded with my swim. The little bay looked as innocent as a millpond, but by the time I was twenty-five feet out and waist-deep in the water, I felt a current against my lower body that nearly swept me off my feet. It was that sudden and strong. As I stood there in one spot, I could feel the sand being excavated from under my feet. This was the first time I had ever experienced a real undertow. I have swum in the Ohio and the Missouri since I was a kid, and though there are many warnings about this danger, I had never felt it. Now, I knew it could be deadly. I suppose that if you stood in this sand long enough, you would eventually disappear.

I walked out of the small bay, and for a while I just sat on the beach enjoying my beer, bathed in the warmth and last light of an incredibly beautiful sunset. I cannot remember ever being so content and free from care.

I stayed on the island five days. Every day seemed better than the last. I read, wrote, swam, explored. I observed the birds and deer and turtles. I tried my hand at fishing, but was happy that I caught nothing, for that would have meant killing, gutting, and cleaning a once-living creature that I really didn't need in order to survive and that I didn't enjoy eating that much anyway. The birds got used to me. The deer, though they never permitted a close approach, at least didn't stampede to the water when I showed myself. The turtles, as is their wont, reacted not at all. They exhibited neither fear nor interest but just sat soaking up warmth, blinking their eyes, and occasionally slipping into the river for a swim, a drink, or whatever they do in the water.

It struck me as ludicrous that much of the life on this island, sentient and otherwise, predated me by millions of years, and yet I was totally convinced that I and my kind were the superior species. If so, I realized, this superiority was not based on strength or the longevity of my species, or the ability to live peacefully with other creatures, including ourselves.

I left my island to continue my journey with great regret. Life cannot not always be so calm and peaceful. And not many of us would want it to be. But I do think it is imperative to the human spirit that there be memories of such magic times. We can sustain ourselves in periods of trouble with the belief that someday we will reexperience those grand and serene moments in our lives.

Manny's Place

There were nights on my trek down the river when I could not deny myself the pleasure of a cold beer, a hot meal, a little human company, and eventually a soft bed. On one such night, after a harrowing 140-mile run down a high but falling, swift, and drift-strewn Mississippi, with these pleasures in mind I pulled into Helena, Arkansas, at about 8:00 P.M. The town was strangely quiet, not a single citizen in sight or a neon light to steer on. I sort of figured that this was just a lull before the good ol' boys showed to liven things up. But as I walked around, Helena appeared to be a ghost town. A last desperate reconnoiter of Main Street did reveal one alternative to early bed. This was a beer joint called Manny's Place.

The inside of this nightspot was about forty feet square, with a ceiling that stretched into a dirty smoky infinity. There were wooden booths on three sides and a small bar on the fourth. The center of the room was occupied by a full-sized pool table overhung by a bright green-shaded bulb. The surface of the table was well patched, the wooden coaming well notched and initialed by countless whittlings. Eight or ten guys lurking in the booths laid a flat suspicious gaze on me that held no hint of friendliness. They made it perfectly clear that bearded strangers weren't welcome in these parts. As they were all wearing "Arkansas Toothpicks"—that is, bowie knives—on their belts, I almost took the hint they were sending out and fled. But my thirst overpowered my cowardice, and I sidled warily over to the bar.

Manny's Place was run by a lady named Belle. I would like to report that she approached me in a friendly manner and said something like, "Howdy, stranger! What'll you have this evening?" But, alas, I must report that it was just the same flat, suspicious stare of the boys in the back booths and a perfunctory, "Yours?"

"Well, ma'am," I said with a smile and a hearty manner and a look that suggested I would be wagging my tail if I were a puppy dog, "I've just had a harrowing day navigating alone in a small open skiff, down a flooded and drift-strewn Mississippi River on my way to New Orleans. I'm seventeen days out of Pittsburgh, and I would like to have the biggest and coldest beer in the house!"

"They all the same, mister," she said, reaching in an antique soft-drink cooler and hoisting out a dripping bottle of beer. And she was right: they was all the same—lukewarm.

Sitting next to me at the bar was a compact little man who introduced himself by the unlikely name of Shelbourne K. Baylor. "S.B.," as he was known to his friends (and he said I was to number myself among them), revealed that he was fifty years old and an off-duty deckhand from a river towboat. Having a background in common, Shelbourne and I became friendly and swapped a few lies about towboating and women and the world in general. He was feisty and forthright, and if his stories of feminine conquest were even half true, he'd been busy as a mink.

There was another person of note in Manny's Place. Her name was Bessie Louise, and she was a winsome young thing. Bessie was the barmaid, waitress, and general all-around object of the ham-handed affections of her male patrons. She was just twenty-one and hadn't been off the farm long enough to realize that Manny's Place wasn't exactly the big time. She leaned against the jukebox and poured out her heart while I drank my second beer. It seemed she was the classic heroine of the country-western ballad. Hers was the old, old story of the wholesome, agrarian lass whose head had been turned and whose good Christian upbringing had been compromised by a fast-talking dry goods drummer from the big city. As she spoke, Bessie moved from the jukebox and leaned against me.

Well, my monopoly on Bessie's attention aroused considerable irritation in Belle, who was paying Bessie to spread herself around a little. But more importantly, as far as my health was concerned, it was causing great anguish among the local boys, who were finding themselves with nothing more to slap than the tabletop. Bessie was mine, but I knew from the rumblings in the back booth that my civil rights were about to be violated as well as my body.

Good old Shelbourne K., carefully attuned to the prospect of violence, knew this also. You don't need a beer can thrown at you to tell when hostilities are about to break out in a beer joint like Manny's; the louder demands for more beer and the tense feeling in the air were sufficient warning. Shelbourne K. was all for the two of us defending my rights to the last drop of blood. "Let's us fight them fellers. I ain't skeered," he said. He pulled back his shirt to reveal a deadly looking little .25 caliber automatic.

I glanced at my small-town Dulcinea and at the boys fixing for a fight. I hated to deprive my new pal of his big moment, but I *was* "skeered," and I had no intention of being pummeled or worse over Bessie Louise that hot July night in Arkansas. Bessie would have to find someone else to help satisfy her hankering to further her education about life in the big city. I said my good nights and sidled warily past the local boys and into the night. I went back to my room unfed, undespoiled, and, most important, uninjured.

I hope that my new friend Shelbourne K. did not pursue his aggressive intentions after his compadre left in such an unseemly hurry. A .25 caliber slug can be deadly to an ordinary person, but might not be much of a stopper when fired into the hide of a 250-pound Arkansas country boy. It would have to go straight into an eyeball or smack dab into the heart. I guess S.B. got out alive. I would hate to think of him ejected from a sweet place like Manny's one piece at a time.

But better him than me.

A Companion Arrives

I awoke one morning just above Natchez and realized that something was missing from this minor odyssey of mine. My son Jim. Of course, he was in school, the bane of all adventurous youngsters, but I never minded taking him out for a short time if something interesting was looming. He was not a brilliant student but always got pretty good grades, and time out of school could also be a learning experience.

I had been selfish: this was *my* trip, and I had wanted solitude. But this was too good to keep all to myself. Jim Boy, as he was known to his mother and sisters, had been my companion on many working trips during my harbor tug days and was respected for his self-contained and hardworking habits. He had served a long, hard apprenticeship and more than deserved to be here with me.

Having him aboard would not be like being saddled with a Little Lord Fauntleroy. Among Jim's river credits was a trip the previous summer as the deckhand and sole crew member aboard a forty-five-foot cruiser being taken by its owner to his home mooring in St. Petersburg, Florida. Though still only twelve years old, Jim had seen the whole lower Mississippi, the Gulf Intracoastal Waterway, and the west coast of Florida.

At Natchez I called his mother and asked that he be shipped by bus to Baton Rouge, where I would pick him up at the bus station. This she did with no qualms, for our children were all very capable and adventurous. I planned to get some food into the inner man and boy and then spend the night at Red's Boat Store, where all marine needs, as well as food and lodging, were available. We would stock up on supplies in the morning and then continue on to New Orleans.

I arrived at Red's Boat Store the next afternoon. Having been out of touch with the world for twenty-three days, I was unaware that Baton Rouge was in the throes of serious civil rights demonstrations and that the National Guard was patrolling the streets with loaded weapons and enforcing a 7:30 P.M. curfew. I spent the day boating around the harbor, seeing things up close that I had previously seen only in passing. Checking with the bus station, I found that Jim Boy was due in at six-thirty. This schedule would give us ample time to walk the mile or so back to the safety of the riverbank before the rigidly enforced curfew shut down the city.

At six-thirty I was at the station. The bus arrived, but Jim did not. The next one would not come in until ten-thirty. I paced around, wondering how this would work out. I sure didn't want us to spend the night in the bus station or to be done in by an overly eager curfew patrol.

Jim Boy arrived on the ten-thirty bus and blithely revealed that he had done some sightseeing in Memphis and had missed the earlier connection. He was too big to spank, but I gave him a good chewing out. He was not at all contrite. In fact, he was excited about the whole adventure, especially when he saw the soldiers out on the darkened street.

We couldn't make it back to the river—no taxis or buses were available, and walking that far after curfew was out of the question. There were no hotels or motels nearby. I had just about resigned myself to the hard wooden seats of the bus station when a baggage clerk told us about Ma's Boarding House three blocks away. We decided to try it. My first instinct was to skulk through back alleys and favor the shadows, but better sense told me that would be an excellent way to get us shot as looters. So Jim and I just marched up to the first patrolman, explained our problem, and an understanding sergeant personally delivered us by jeep.

Ma's Boarding House was a huge, three-story, dingy, rickety clapboard building with practically no lights showing. Those that did show had the distinctive, depressing quality of low-watt bulbs seen through pulled-down, age-yellowed blinds. All around us was darkness and deep shadow. The nearest street light was half a block away, and its feeble light only intensified the shadows, creating the feeling that we were on a Hitchcock set and that to enter the house would result in a Hitchcock fate. The silence and total absence of life were oppressive, and I began to wish that we had opted for the bus station. I found the doorbell, through no fault of the twenty-five-watt bulb overhead, and rang.

We heard footsteps, ponderous and slow. The door opened, and there, framed not in light but only in gloom, stood Ma herself. She would have been a fit mate for Uncle Festus: hennaed hair, rouged cheeks, dressed in a housedress and mules. Behind her a dark hallway stretched back to a once grand staircase. The only light in the hall was a small lamp on a night stand containing the register, or perhaps it was a list of victims.

"Howdy, honey," Ma said, though which one of us she was addressing, I never knew. "You all looking for a room?"

I said we were, and she said, "My, that little feller looks all in. Kinda pale, ain't he?"

In fact, Jim Boy *was* pale but not from fatigue. This place was the wrong kind of excitement for him.

The room cost $4.00 and at half the price would have been expensive. It was bare, high-ceilinged, and illuminated by one naked forty-watt bulb. There was one closet that I didn't care even to look into and a badly painted dresser with a cracked mirror. The bathroom was down the hall and was occupied when we decided to brave it. I waited ten minutes, then knocked on the door. Shortly after, it opened, and a wizened old man, looking like a half-starved vampire, tottered down the hall. The trickle of water that came out of the faucet into the rust-and-grime-stained tub precluded a relaxing soak. The sink was little better and the towels out of the question.

Jim and I approached the swaybacked bed, whose sheets and pillowcases indicated that clean linen was not a tradition of the house. We pulled the blanket back over the sheets, and Jim lay down kind of rigid-like in order to expose as little of himself as possible to the bedclothes. I lay down beside him, but the extra weight was too much for the bed. It sagged so badly that our bottoms almost touched the floor, and we rolled together like two in a hammock.

We had left a call for 7:00 A.M., and after a restless night awoke on our own at eight. The price of the room included breakfast, and despite all, we intended to avail ourselves of this bonus. A lanky fellow in the kitchen sporting a toothpick and a dirty apron informed us we were too late.

Ma was nowhere to be seen, so we were unable to bid her farewell. With sore backs and profound relief, we made our way in the bright sunlight back to the happy world of boats and water.

Last Lapse

After our harrowing night at Ma's Boarding House, Jim Boy and I loaded the boat and decided to tour the Baton Rouge harbor for half a day to look at the places we had both seen only in passing. There were many oceangoing ships, all tankers, anchored in the middle of the river, awaiting turns to load out or discharge cargo. How the huge Mississippi River tows could thread their way between them was beyond belief.

I explained to Jim how the ships arrived, through the delta passes of the Mississippi at Pilot Town south of New Orleans, where they were taken over by professional American river pilots. Bless his heart, Jim never acted blasé about anything I told him. Though he had seen all this before, he allowed me to lecture as though I were showing him something new and wondrous. He remained like that for many years; not until young manhood did he decide that the old man no longer required a "Gee Whiz, Dad!" to make him feel like a proper father and tutor.

He was an unfailingly good companion for the days we had left together. He handled the boat with great skill and never approached a possibly dangerous place that he was curious about without asking permission. I would pretend to weigh the situation and invariably say, "Sure, Captain Jim, but be careful." Jim did not chatter like a magpie, but if he had a question, he never hesitated to ask it, and my answers had to make sense and be accurate. There was no fluffing him off. He was too bright and discerning for that. I do not believe that I could ever love that boy more than I did in those days together. He was so healthy, so handsome, so much his own man. I was truly proud of him and would become more so as the trip and then the years progressed.

Before we knew it, it was late afternoon in Baton Rouge, so we decided to spend another night on the riverbank near Red's Boat Store and get an early start in the morning. We'd be departing from about Mile 240, and New Orleans is at Mile 90. The city is located ninety miles upriver from the Passes, which is Mile 0, AHP, meaning "Ahead of the Passes." These passes are part of the Mississippi delta and allow access to the river from the Gulf by means of the Main Pass, Southeast Pass, and Southwest Pass. Mileage is counted upstream on the Lower Miss, whereas most rivers, including the Ohio, count mileage downriver from their source.

The first leg of our journey together took us to Live Oak Manor just below Destrehan, Louisiana. Jim Boy did most of the steering that day. I wasn't tired of it, but he enjoyed it, and I enjoyed just watching the scenery. Passing three upbound tows, he gave them a good wide berth and had sense enough not to cut in behind them until their mighty wheel-wash had subsided. The shores were lined with stone dikes that help control the river depth and channel direction. For the most part they were deep enough under the water to be no danger to us. Nevertheless, Jim took no chances; he continually checked the chart and stayed well outside their extension into the river.

"Dad, we should do this again," he remarked often enough to make sure that I got the message.

"We will if time and tide, finances, and Atropos, permit."

"What do you mean tide? There's no tide in the river. And who is Atropos?"

"Right you are about the tides, my man. Merely a figure of speech.

Does the phrase 'time and tide wait for no man' mean anything to you?"

"No," he said.

"Well, we will let that go by for the time being. Atropos was one of the demigoddesses of Greek mythology, one of a trio called the Fates. Her job was to cut the mortal string that ends a human's sojourn on earth. So by invoking her I meant that if we do not anger the immortals and live long enough, we could do this trip again."

He thought about what I said for moment, then said, "For a dumb old river rat, you sound pretty smart sometimes."

"Just showing off, my boy. So while you think about that, just get us safely down this here old river." And he did.

Besides Oak Manor, we saw numerous other plantation riverfronts with majestic trees hung with Spanish moss and flanking the dirt roads leading to the mansions, or what was left of them. In the old days these plantations had been regular stops for steamboats to load or unload passengers and all the store-bought necessities of life as well as the produce of the plantations, mostly cotton, for these isolated abodes of the wealthy southern planters. Now, of course, a lot of these places are all fixed up and open to tourists, but when Jim Boy and I saw them, they had mostly gone the way of Rhett Butler and Scarlett O'Hara.

That night, as on all other nights in this almost tropical part of the river, the mosquitoes were positively fierce, and I would venture to say that they weighed about ten to the pound. There was no sleeping outside the tent to get relief from the heat and mugginess, and it was a mite crowded in there for two, even though one was not full grown.

We awoke early and, despite missing a few pints of blood, were able to fix breakfast and get under way. We could tell we were getting close to the great history-and-mystery-shrouded metropolis of New Orleans, for towboat traffic picked up, and refineries and other industries lined the shore. Then I spotted Wagaman Light and knew we had reached the outskirts of the city. There were ships tied to the wharves on both sides of the river, loading and discharging cargo, as well as barge fleets. At the Poydras Street Wharf next to the foot of Canal Street was the banana mecca of the United States. We passed the steamer *President*, a huge excursion boat and the sister ship to the now long-gone *Island Queen* on which my father had served as mate. Then we made a crossover to Algiers Point, a sharp short bend and, at 268 feet, the deepest spot in the inland waterways. We proceeded down through the anchored ships at Quarantine Area and made a long crossover to the entrance of the Industrial Lock and into the Industrial Canal that would take us into Lake

The towboat *Ralph E. Plagge* at New Orleans

Pontchartrain with its huge municipal marina. Here the marina manager allowed us to tie up for the few days we had left. We'd see New Orleans and decide whether to sell the boat and equipment.

Jim Boy was tired and pretty much overwhelmed by all he'd seen that day, and though the promise of exploring this fascinating city was exciting to him, I could tell that he was sorry the river trip was over. We showered at the marina, put on clean clothes, and caught a bus to the city, where we booked a room at the Cornstalk Hotel in the French Quarter. We stopped at Felix's Oyster House, where I tried to get Jim to eat a raw oyster, but he wasn't having any of that. I ate a dozen myself while Jim settled for a fish sandwich.

We passed several days exploring, and Jim really learned to love the historic old quarter. This was before many of the old buildings were demolished and pseudo-French motels and office buildings replaced them.

We took the famous St. Charles trolley ride several times through the Garden District, visited the zoo, and rode the streetcar named Desire. We took three cruises on the *President*. I met old friends from Mt. Adams: Doc Hawley, then playing the calliope on the *President* and now a steamboat captain, and the irrepressible Betty Blake of the Green Line Steamers.

On our return to the marina I found no taker for the boat; however, the harbormaster introduced us to a truck driver who agreed to haul our equipment, the boat, her motor, Jim, and me to Louisville for sixty dollars. I grabbed the deal. At Louisville, I called my friend Mary, who agreed to meet us with a car at Schmidt Field, a boat launching facility in Cincinnati's East End. I put the boat back in the water, and we headed for home.

Mary was waiting when we arrived, along with my dog Dia. Mary looked so sweet in shorts and a hooded sweater that my heart overflowed with affection; I pulled in to the bank and jumped out of the boat. It was a toss up as to who was the most excited—Mary, me, Jim, or Dia. God, it was good to see our hometown and our loved ones again.

Thirty-one days and 2,000 miles of river, and we were finally home! It had been a great trip, the best part being when Jim Boy came aboard and we had so much fun together. We had gained a new camaraderie and mutual respect.

Next day, Jim went back to school, and after a couple of days of reorganizing my life, I went back to my regular work on the towboats. I was three days late, but Bill took it cheerfully. He knew I would do the same for him. I did not leave the Ohio River and towboating again for any length of time until I left for good around 1980—except for one period when I built my own tugboat and worked the New Orleans harbor. That was my next adventure.

New Orleans Harbor
1973-1974

Vulcan, a Little Tug
That Could and Did

There is no explaining why a man would want to build his own boat and operate his own river business. Yet I did just that. It must have been growing pains. About two years after my trip to New Orleans in my small aluminum boat, I got the urge to buy large amounts of steel and weld them into my own harbor tug. I quit the job I had then as a towboat pilot and captain and found a weedy lot at a marina out near Coney Island to build her on. I got the space in exchange for repair work on the marina's floats. I put my last dollar and a lot of my sweat and Jimmy's sweat into her. My wife and I had reconciled at the time, and she reluctantly got behind the project, along with a bank that was impressed with the model we presented. We borrowed money to buy parts and materials. The engines were two junked International truck engines, which we rebuilt and were rated at about 200 horsepower each.

A good friend of mine named Paul Townsend helped me and Jim Boy build her. We spent a year on her, working twelve and fifteen hours a day in sometimes bitter cold. She was a twin screw with an unusual, in those days, catamaran hull that limited the engine space but gave her far better backing power. Her measurements were 30 feet long by 16 feet wide. When the major work was done, we lettered her name, *Vulcan*, on her stern and pilothouse. I am avid reader of mythology: Greek, Roman, Norse, and others. Greek is my favorite, but I chose the simpler Roman name *Vulcan* because the Greek *Hephaestus* presented too many spelling and pronunciation problems; both are gods of fire and the forge. And who could pronounce Hephaestus, much less paint all those letters on a small boat?

On a cold, sunny day in March we proceeded to launch the *Vulcan*. We all felt very proud as we saw her rise into the air on a boat lift that held her like a cradle and eased her into the water. The smoke that came from the engines was a gratifying sight as she roared into life. She looked awfully small out on the big river, and she had looked so big when we welded her hull and hammered on her roof. Could this tiny tug actually represent a year's work?

When I got behind the sticks I found that the *Vulcan* handled well and had great astern power thanks to her catamaran hull configuration.

My tugboat, the *Vulcan*,
under construction

Left, the *Vulcan* in profile. *Below*,
the pilothouse

I was happy with her. I would be my own man, free of dispatchers and bosses, responsible only to the demands I inflicted on myself. I also hoped that running my own operation would increase my income.

I spent a very hardworking year with the *Vulcan* in the Cincinnati harbor. We towed barges for various companies, repaired them, did hatch repairs, took care of minor hull damage, replaced deck hardware such as timberheads, ratchets, and cavels, installed new barge towing knees, and painted barges. I once took nine empties from the Beckford power plant to Miami Fort, and Captain John Beattey said over the radio he couldn't figure out what was pushing the load; looked to him like a telephone booth on a raft. Eventually I lengthened the *Vulcan* six feet; I judged that her stern was too short and that she needed a little more ass.

I was very busy and paying my bills. Sometimes we worked seven days a week and sometimes were called in the middle of the night to work on barges due to leave our area the next day.

The following spring, a major barge line for whom I did work as an independent contractor asked me if I would be interested in working for them at their New Orleans facility. Was I interested! On my trip down south in the little boat with my son, I had found New Orleans an exciting place, and the work would be very different from what I was accustomed to. With my wife's and family's blessing, I put my affairs in order and set sail south with the *Vulcan* wired up to a brand-new 4,000-horsepower towboat belonging to the company. I worked my way to our destination by doing the bigger boat's tug work at various points along the way.

As on the previous trip, I got my first glimpse of oceangoing ships at Baton Rouge. I was in the company towboat's pilothouse kibitzing with the captain. It was just a glimpse because we were running in near shut-out fog, and these ships were all anchored in the middle of the river, their ghostly shapes barely visible but clearly indicated on the radar. Their presence didn't deter our nerveless captain. Pushing a seventeen-barge tow, he threaded his way through this gaggle of ships without turning a hair. I was mightily impressed, and though I didn't like him very much, I respected the hell out of him—the more so after this demonstration of skill and classic riverman cool.

Just above the Huey Long Bridge, the gateway to New Orleans, I bade him and his crew farewell and headed for Point Landing, which at that time was probably the largest tugboat and fleeting operation on the inland waterways. There I took on fuel and decided to take a good long look at my new area of operations.

It was like nothing I'd ever experienced on the Ohio with our strictly domestic craft. Ships from countries all over the world (except the Soviet Union and Red China, with whom we did not do business at the time) were moored to the docks on both sides of the river, and there were barge fleets everywhere. River traffic was so busy that there were traffic lights controlling the main harbor, bounded by the Huey Long Bridge at the upper limit and Algiers Point at the lower. The first traffic light, for downbound vessels, was on top of a grain elevator, complete with control room and operator. The second light controlling upriver traffic was perched atop the Domino Sugar warehouse. The lights were huge but patterned just like city traffic lights: red for stop, amber for wait, green for go. Running a red light brought the risk of collision with oncoming traffic that could seem to block the river from bank to bank. The Port Authority issued warnings, citations, and fines for violations.

The harbor was busy all the time with seagoing ships, towboats, tugboats, ferries, excursion boats, and often the huge deep-draft, steam-powered fireboat, the *Deluge*. This vessel put out a wake so powerful that it could unface a tugboat from its tow. I learned to head for the spaces between moored ships when I saw her coming.

My deal with the barge line that had brought me down to New Orleans fell through, but I soon made an arrangement with a fleeting outfit called East Bank Marine Service, which was located on the New Orleans side of the Mississippi just below the Huey Long Bridge and about nine miles upriver from Canal Street, the heart of the city. It was a large barge fleeting harbor but had no tugboat. I furnished the tug, and East Bank provided the jobs. Working with a likable Cajun named Vic, the fleet boss and tankerman, we delivered to the big towboats sundry items such as newspapers, girlie magazines, fresh water, spare parts, and food. We towed the Gulf Oil Company's fuel barge, *Miss Kitty*, out to them for refueling in mid-river. Remember, the line-haul boats can't stop for much, and we would pump fuel into them as we both proceeded up or down the river.

Working with Obbie, a personable black man I hired as my deckhand for special jobs, I also towed a larger barge for Gulf Oil, used for supplying oil to the oceangoing ships that made my little tug look like a toy. Our job was to "bunker" the ships—that is, pump aboard the heavy "Bunker C." oil used to fire boilers and as fuel for certain types of diesel engines.

We would get our orders from the oil company that went something like this: Deliver so many drums of oil to such and such a ship registered in the Republic of —— (whatever new name a country I thought I

A tugboat and midstream-fueling barge (similar to the *Miss Kitty*). The small boat will tie up alongside a long-haul boat and deliver, while both are still under way, not only fuel and lube oil but potable water, groceries, mail, and newspapers (courtesy of Dorothy Weil).

was familiar with had acquired). "Where is she?" I would ask, knowing what the answer would be.

"At the ship quarantine anchorage," the dispatcher would reply.

Since there were usually several dozen ships at that anchorage below Algiers Point, I would have to navigate among them, sometimes a matter of hours, until I found the one I was looking for.

The next problem would be waking up the crew. My boat horn seldom sufficed, since there were horns blowing in New Orleans harbor all the time. We would usually be reduced to going in alongside the ship, close enough for the deckhand to rap her hull smartly several times with a sledgehammer. This stratagem generally brought results: either curses and shaken fists, or a pleasant wave from a crew member who would then wander away and forget all about us.

Eventually we would get someone's attention and establish our reason for being there. Because of the variety of languages spoken on the ships, sign language was often necessary, and I found that the greatest degree of understanding, not to mention attention, was achieved by my making a circle of my left thumb and forefinger and pretending to strive mightily, with accompanying grimaces, to push my right forefinger through the opening. Signs of interest would begin to appear. Then I would point to a drum of oil, mime dipping my finger into it, and dem-

The *Irinio*, an oceangoing
vessel of the type I
"bunkered" in New
Orleans

A closer look at the *Irinio*, showing its "Jacob's ladder." A tiny tug like mine can be
seen at lower right.

onstrate how easily it now penetrated the circle and worked in and out. The crew would commence grinning and clapping their hands. I think they thought we were a new style of American bumboat with a cargo of loose ladies.

But even if we had been, there would have been no sin perpetrated that afternoon for just about the time the first man started down the Jacob's ladder, the ship's chief engineer would finally show up and the work would begin. First came the mooring lines, huge hawsers that could have secured the *Mighty Mo.* Then a lighter line to pull the oil hose up a thirty-five-foot steel ship's hull, over the rail, and across the deck to the headers (valves of the oil tanks). When the loading was finally done, the engineering officer would show up again, and he and I would start on the paperwork. And there sure was a mess of it. All of this would have been difficult enough had we spoken the same language, but trying to do it in two languages often reduced the procedure to an Abbott and Costello routine.

Home base, the East Bank Marine Service, was seldom restful either. Once, an enormous mass of drift got lodged across the head of a nearby fleet and caused a hundred-barge breakaway. This huge gathering of uncontrolled floating stock came very near to wiping clean of ships all the docks down the New Orleans waterfront. It took the combined efforts of thirty-two tugboats, of which the *Vulcan* was one, to get this mess stopped and shoved into the bank, and that accomplished only after the arrival of a 3,200 horsepower towboat.

At the harbor, I shared a tired old trailer atop the levee with Vic, whose hobby, it turned out, was other men's wives. Nevertheless, I loved the time in New Orleans; the city was exciting, and I learned that the only two subjects that transcend all language barriers are sex and money—in what order, I'm still not sure.

Bab-El on the Old Miss

With ships in the harbor from every country, New Orleans was like the Tower of Babel. Trying to deal with all the world's languages was never easy. I had many near misses with other boats because of misunderstood passing arrangements. I had problems over dollars promised for towing work (with me somehow always on the short end), arrivals at the wrong places at the wrong times, and oil or water pumped into the wrong hole because the identification plates did not say "water" or "oil" but were labeled with any number of words indecipherable by me. I couldn't help wishing the whole world would speak English—but, then, the Cajuns were speaking English and I couldn't understand them either.

When the language barrier came close to costing me my life, or at best a severe pummeling at the hands of an irate chief engineer from across the globe, that was too much. In one instance, the threat was a chief engineer, who was swole up like an apoplectic blowfish, shaking his fist under my nose and shouting in what I took to be Italian (since he was on an Italian ship). I vowed then and there that if I got out of this situation alive, I was also going to get out of New Orleans and head back to the good old Midwest.

It all started with an oil company dispatcher calling me with orders to deliver fifty drums of oil to a ship named SS *Cosa Nostra*, or something like that. I know that the chief and his henchmen looked tough enough to be cast in a gangster flick.

This time, miracle of miracles, the dispatcher knew where the ship was: "She's loading grain at the elevator at Nine Mile Point." That was nearby, and it wasn't long before we were alongside, tied off, and pumping oil. The weather was fine, things were going well, and everyone was cheerful, including the chief. Soon the job was finished; we got the hoses back aboard the barge, and the chief and I went to his quarters to do the paperwork.

These transactions, for some reason, involve vast numbers of documents. Each of us had to sign our names many times, he as the agent of the shipowner, and I as agent of the oil company. I spread the work out on his table; he offered me a drink. I started signing and indicating that he should do the same. He reached out, took the pen from my hand, and said something in Italian. I didn't understand.

The New Orleans skyline from mid-river. A fuel barge is returning home from its job; the towboat is heading for one of the many barge fleets in the harbor (courtesy of DorothyWeil).

He tried again. By then he was getting louder and red in the face. I still failed to understand.

He tried a gesture meaning "gimme," rubbing his fingertips together, counting out money on his palm. I got the significance of that right away but failed to see what it had to do with me. He was beginning to swell up now, and I was beginning to get alarmed. He picked up the pen and made a dollar sign on one piece of paperwork, then pointed to the words "fifty drums," held up one finger, then wrote "50" behind the dollar sign.

The light began to dawn. Apparently the sales agent had promised him a $50 kickback for the sale. In perfect Italian, I said, "Me no gotta de feefty dollars! Me no get money from boss man."

"You tella the big lie," I think he said, "you keepa the money yourself." With that he swept about half the papers onto the floor and reached for my shirt front.

Dodging his hand, I screeched in alarm, "I tella you, I no gotta de money!" I pointed to his phone and to the telephone number of the agent. "You calla this fella," I said.

Well, he did. He discovered that the agent had other arrangements for the payoff. With that, the chief became his old friendly self, helped me pick up the papers, and signed without further ado. "You gooda boy. No steala da money," he said and slapped me on the back.

"And you, Chief," I said in perfect clear English and with a smile, "are a creep as well as a lucky man. I'd have cut your ears off if you had got hold of me." Which I wouldn't have, since I had no knife or stomach for blood.

He escorted me to the Jacob's ladder that goes down the ship's side, smiling and back-patting all the way, and soon I was headed for home.

I had a few choice words for that dispatcher, and I leave you with the good advice that if you ever decide to do business on the New Orleans waterfront, you had better be able to speak about eighteen languages. And carry a pistol.

Old China Hand—Out

The observation that sex and money are the only two subjects that transcend all linguistic barriers applies even to the Chinese, who speak the language most foreign to the Occidental ear. In my case it applied especially to the Chinese, for it was they who had ushered me, as a seventeen-year-old U.S. Navy sailor, out of the age of innocence in a Shanghai "sandokan" and who have, in the ensuing years, lightened my purse on numerous other occasions.

This, of course, does not include transactions with Chinese restaurants, that have given me my money's worth, especially the one who threw in a parboiled cricket with my chow mein at no extra cost. When I discovered this premium viand, it was half gone, including one drumstick, so I concluded that I had eaten that much of him. This experience led me to the conclusion that, since I am still alive, ingesting crickets won't kill you. I passed, however, on the balance of the parboiled Jiminy, as well as that day's chow mein.

Since the various larcenous depredations on my purse were usually accomplished with my cooperation, I hold no grudge; the Orientals simply outwitted me. Which doesn't say too much for their smarts, since I am a classical example of what old P.T. Barnum once said was "born every minute." But my victimization at the hands of certain Chinese in New Orleans still smarts, because it hit me when my purse was really hurting.

My deckhand, Obbie, and I had been ordered to deliver fifty drums of special lubrication oil to a Chinese Nationalist ship awaiting its turn to load at the ship wharves. They were not to get the drums, only the oil, so it was necessary to pump out each of the barrels stacked on the deck of the fuel barge. The pump was a very powerful and efficient mechanism that would darn near suck the bottom out of a drum; after all, it had to push heavy oil thirty-five to forty feet straight up. Each time a drum was emptied, it was necessary in the transfer process to hold a large rag over the pipe to keep oil from dripping all over the deck.

Obbie was tending to this work, and I cautioned him that whatever he did, he must not let go of the rag. After two and a half drums, that is precisely what he did. But I must say that he was dead game. That pump sucked about half of his arm up the tube, and since he was faced with the choice of losing the rag and an arm or just the rag, he opted for the latter, and the cloth immediately jammed the pump.

This was a real calamity. I had no proper tools, we had no spare pumps, and we were seventeen miles from the refinery with forty-seven and a half drums to go. My only recourse was to get the pump repaired aboard the ship. So I explained the problem as best as I could to the engineering officer. He finally got the message and said something incomprehensible, finishing up with an oily smile and a glint in his eye, which I should have recognized from past experience meant he was calculating to smoke a buck out of the Round Eyes.

We got the pump disconnected from the deck of the barge, up the side of the ship, and down into the engine room. The chief rattled off a few phrases to a mechanic nearby, which probably meant, "You fix pump," for that is what he commenced doing. He also must have told him something else, because that fellow was grinning from ear to ear.

In less than twenty minutes the mechanic had that pump repaired and ready to go. I was just as happy as could be, because I calculated that I could still make it back to the landing in time for a tray of crabs and a couple of cold beers. Obbie and I started toward the workbench to fetch the pump, but before we reached it the chief and the mechanic literally threw themselves over it as if to say, "You'll have to kill us first." Actually, what the chief said was, "Twenny-fi' dolla'. You pay twenny-fi' dolla' first." The mechanic was no longer smiling, and I noticed that he had not turned loose of a three-foot torque wrench.

Now, $25 was an exorbitant charge for the work done, and further, most people on the river would have repaired the pump for free, especially when it was needed to complete a job. I gave that chief a good Anglo-Saxon four-letter piece of my mind, which Lord knows I couldn't spare, but of course he didn't understand. So, not having any choice, I gave him "twenny-fi' dolla'," which I also couldn't spare. The $1.13 cents I had left sure wasn't going to buy me any crabs and beer.

Language barrier or no, the Chinese have taken, among other lesser chattels, two very precious possessions from me. The first I didn't really mind. One has to lose it somewhere. But that $25 still rankles. One of these days I am going to get it back, and I do not care if it's the silverware from a local Chinese restaurant.

Ships That Pass in the Night

It was 2:00 A.M., and I was just crawling into bed aboard my tugboat when the telephone Klaxon blared from the office trailer atop the levee. I groaned, muttered a few obscenities, and resolved to ignore it. But whoever it was seemed equally resolved not to be ignored. Besides, the call might mean some business for me, which I could always use, even after spending the last seventeen hours refueling a Chinese Nationalist ship down at the quarantine anchorage.

I put a slicker on over my underwear, slipped on my boots, and headed for the trailer. Good Lord, it was a bad night. The river was high and swift, and the rain was coming down in torrents. Great herds of thunder rolled across the sky, their path starkly lit by flashes of lightning that dramatically silhouetted the spiderwork girders of the Huey Long Bridge a quarter-mile upriver. I began to hope the call was a wrong number.

But no such luck. It was Pete, the night dispatcher.

"Hey, old buddy, how ya doin'?" he asked, not really caring.

A typical New Orleans harbor tug
(courtesy of Dorothy Weil)

"Whatcha want, Pete?" I asked, with no enthusiasm in my voice.

"Got a tug over at Avondale Shipyards trying to get a barge out of the fleet to take downriver. But he's too big to get at it. I need you to go over and pull it out for him. He'll take it from you midstream, and you can go back to bed."

I knew it wouldn't do any good to grumble, and Pete sent a lot of business my way. Still, in a final futile effort to get out of leaving my warm bed, I said, "'Sides, Pete, I ain't got a deckhand."

"No problem. Just use the man off the other boat." He had me there, so I said okay and hung up.

As I headed away from the landing, I could barely see the lights of the Avondale Shipyards, which was only a mile upriver and the brightest place in the New Orleans harbor. The current was running a good five to six miles per hour, and I was sure glad all I had to do was dig that barge out and then let the other feller take it down the river.

Avondale's whole riverfront in the 1970s was cluttered up with submarines, destroyers, freighters, seagoing barges, and offshore oil rigs. Where the last oil rig was moored, the barge fleet began. They were tied in there five wide and seven long, all empties awaiting repairs, and as

Pete had said, there was not enough room for the larger tug to get between the fleet and the oil rig. Being a little shorter, my boat was just able to make it.

The barge we were after was about 350 feet long and 52 feet wide, and was tied off on the outer upstream end of the fleet. That was a real break; I wouldn't have to tear the whole fleet apart to get at it. I faced down on the barge, and the deckhand from the other tug put on the wires.

I took off, trying to hold the head in and back the stern out into the river and upstream a bit, or even a lot if the little tug would do it. This would give me a lot of extra room above the bridge piers when I started to top (turn) it end for end. But I had no sooner started the stern out and upriver when the current poured into the V-shaped space this move created, and I had to abandon hope of backing into that current. The barge started to top around long before I wanted it to. I had hoped to be able to steer it below the bridge piers before attempting the turn around, but the current was just too strong.

Still, this was really not much of a problem. We had a thousand feet between us and the bridge. I just had to let her go ahead and top out and then top her again. This would put the boat at the fleet end of the barge and the barge bow pointing toward the New Orleans side of the river. We could then "come ahead" into the space between the piers, drop downstream sideways and buy another mile in which to get her pointed in the right direction, and hold her steady with the engines, allowing the other boat to "face down" on the barge and be on his way. On his way, that is, after my boat "unfaced" (turned loose) and headed for home and blessed bed.

So I was feeling pretty good about the whole thing and calculated that I would be pounding my pillow in about thirty minutes. That's when the complication in this little drama came steaming around Twelve Mile Point and straight down on my piece of river. I didn't hear him call because my radio was off. Inexcusable lapse of good sense! I didn't see him because visibility was down to a quarter-mile. This thing that was about to age me ten years was the SS *Manhattan*, one of the early 105-foot-wide, 125-ton supertankers, loaded down with oil. There was no way for him to stop and there was no place for him to maneuver. He was about to slice right through me and my barge, still crosswise in the middle of the black, stormy Mississippi River, and I still hadn't seen him.

It was about then that, just to follow good procedure, I quit thinking about the joys of slumber and, like any good riverman who's been short-circuited for a while, took a good look around. "All clear," I thought to myself, and then took a second good look out of the port pilothouse window.

Right at that moment, the *Manhattan* pilot cracked his big searchlight on me and turned on all the other lights on the ship. I saw the biggest, blackest, ugliest sight there ever was. He was 300 yards away and coming fast. His huge white bow wave was foaming and tumbling back into the black night beyond, and he was zeroed in somewhere along the last third of my barge.

I jammed the throttles so hard ahead they about came off in my hands, and that little boat commenced striving her heart out, as though she too recognized the danger. I kept my eyes on the east bank and the bridge pier, my mind on willing a few more horses out of the engines and pretending that the ship was just a figment of my imagination. I knew he had to be getting close, but I just couldn't look, even though in retrospect I have to say that if he was going to hit, it would have been the most spectacular "last sight" I would ever see.

As you might guess by now, he did miss me, though I could have struck a match off his hull as he went past. And when his bow wave caught us, my little boat almost stood on her nose. I went sailing halfway through the front window; only my death grip on the throttles kept me from going all the way. About then, up loomed the bridge pier. I could not possibly stop her, so we just kept driving full ahead.

While I was waiting for the river gods to decide what to do about me, I spoke up on my own behalf: "Fellers, you let me out of this night alive, and I promise never to come back. I'll just get me a nice job in a library somewhere, and not bother you ever again." I guess they must have heard me, because we did miss that bridge pier. But we sure didn't miss the levee, and once more I made a right sudden trip out the front window.

When peace and quiet once again reigned on the lower Mississippi, that barge was parked halfway up the levee. I stood all a-tremble, staring out into the night and counting my lucky stars. Then I heard footsteps, and who should come sauntering down that barge and out of the rain but the deckhand off the other boat who had helped in the facing-up. I hadn't even known he was aboard but had expected him to stay on the fleet and be picked up by his own boat. He had had one wild ride this night.

"Well, we got that barge cleared up, didn't we?" he said. And we just stood there grinning at each other.

The Odd Couple

Vic the Cajun and I lived together atop the levee for almost a year, in a little twenty-foot trailer that rocked perilously in the wind and leaked when it rained. There was a rough path that led up to it on the landward slope of the levee, and to the riverward there was a spit of land that extended about a hundred yards out into the river. Above, below, and all around this minipeninsula, part of the East Bank Marine Service, were moored dozens of barges. I and my tug boat, the *Vulcan*, furnished tug work; Vic was the fleetmaster of the harbor and the tankerman on its mid-stream refueling barge, the *Miss Kitty*.

Vic and I shared expenses, thus saving money. As the weather grew rainy and disagreeable, I could no longer live on my boat; it was rather cramped to begin with, and the expense of heating and lighting it by means of the generator was out of sight.

Vic was a handsome, wiry, amiable sort of fellow. Though tough, with a strong penchant for trouble, he was not into any form of domestic hostility, and he and I got along very well. We were both fastidious about our persons, when work permitted, and about our living space. I did the cleaning and tended the little flower garden. Vic did the cooking, and I did the dishes. We worked hard and were happy in our little home.

We had a lot of adventures together on the river. Vic was with me when the face wire on the tug broke and almost sank her, and he was with me when we returned thirty miles down the Mississippi in a fog with a gasoline barge in tow and no radar. We went sailing right on by the landing, and when the fog lifted, found ourselves eight miles below the home fleet.

We also had adventures on dry land. Of an evening we would venture down the leeward side of the levee, drawn by the bright lights of the honky-tonks. I can only attribute these occasions to bad judgment on my part. Vic had a magnetic personality. By that I mean he attracted trouble. He had a positive genius for being attracted by and attractive to married women. His need was like that of the moth to the flame, and could have been just as fatal.

Living on the riverbank is not for the fainthearted. Some mighty tough gentlemen frequent the waterfront bars, and since most seafarers suspect their wives of being something less than chaste in their absence, they are mighty thin-skinned about interlopers.

I have to say that over the years I have survived some mighty tough dives, and except when I was young and smart-assed from too much "loud mouth," have for the most part suffered no serious wounds. The secret is to mind your own business, avoid eye contact with the local Mike Fink wannabes, try to give the impression that picking on you might well be more painful than profitable, and, above all, stay away from other fellers' womenfolk. About the only exception to my good luck was when I once turned my head at the wrong time and exposed the old pearly whites to a wayward beer bottle, which, though not meant for me, nevertheless reduced the said pearly whites by one, upper dead center. But accidents will happen, and I bore the thrower no ill will, especially since said thrower was a woman of monumental proportions. Fortunately for her, I have always had a policy of never hitting women, and, most important, this policy included those who could stomp me into a pile of rubble.

With Vic, I was exposed to all the things that I knew better than to do in a bar. One could certainly suggest, with considerable logic, that if I had wanted to stay out of trouble, I should have stayed out of bars when in the company of Vic. I would then have avoided the risk of being considered an accomplice to his peccadilloes and therefore equally guilty in the eyes of outraged husbands—and deserving of the same stern and painful retribution. But I reject guilt by association, even if it hurts.

One might also suggest that as a married man I shouldn't even have entered bars of low repute, replete with ladies of similar standing, married or otherwise. They are no place for a faithful husband, even one suffering from an acute case of prolonged celibacy. But as we all know, temptation is ever nigh, and this is especially true when one's spouse is a thousand miles away.

But life on the river is a tough and lonely life, and when a riverman gets some time off after two or three days of nonstop work, he tends to want to blow off a little steam. So I must admit that, danger or no, I more than willingly accompanied Vic on his evening excursions.

One night we chose the Cotton Club, a popular haunt, and Vic was as usual on the trail of a perhaps discontented but nevertheless very married woman. She sat nearby with a formidable-looking gent whom I, counting on Vic's unerring instincts, took to be her husband. Pretty soon she and Vic commenced rolling their eyeballs at each other like Helen and Paris on his first night in Sparta.

I can't say that the modern Menelaus was aware of this optical fore-play between his wife and the scourge of happy homes, but he sure be-came aware of some vague threat to his wedded bliss when Vic asked her to dance, not once, but several times, and she accepted, not once but every time he asked her.

I could see a minor epic developing here, which moved me to muse that when that inevitable time came when Vic failed to get out the win-dow of a lady friend's house in time, the least tribute we could pay him would be a eulogy chiseled on his tombstone in Homeric meter.

The husband of Vic's dancing partner was beginning to feel the ant-lers on his brow, and though the lady's face would never launch a thou-sand ships, it was about to launch a 1959 Pontiac, a motorcycle, and six .38 caliber bullets.

I just drank my beer and calculated the whereabouts of the exits, covers, and concealments, including the men's john. A very poor choice. I could see myself dead or dying face down in the urinal.

Along about the middle of the fourth quadrille to which he hadn't been invited, the husband had had enough. With a roar that would have caused Stentor to resign as herald of the Greeks and a Viking to throw down his sword, he rushed onto the dance floor, reduced his lady to an undigni-fied heap, and said to Vic, "You bleep, bleep, little Cajun Bleep! I'm gonna blow your head off!" With that, he headed for the side door in a dead run, presumably to fetch the hardware required for the decapitation.

Vic hesitated only a minute, obviously torn between a chivalrous need to restore the lady to her feet and a desire to retain his brain and the box it came in.

Sorry to say the nobler sentiments came in a poor second that evening, and he headed for the front door, grabbing my motorcycle keys on the way out.

I wasn't far behind him and arrived outside just in time to see my beloved and sole means of transportation headed down the pike with a beat-up Pontiac in hot pursuit.

Our landing was only about a quarter of a mile away from that some-what less-than-southern-gentlemanly confrontation at the tavern. In the good old days Vic would have been rapped smartly alongside the jowls with a pair of gloves and expected to show up the next morning with a rapier or dueling pistol. Not, of course, that he would have been there. Vic's honor did not extend to getting his liver spitted or in this case his head removed for the sake of any lady, even one of greater comeliness and virtue than the one in question.

I was a pretty fast runner in those days, but there was no way I could keep up on the straightaway with a Honda cycle and a Pontiac bent respectively on survival and vengeance. So I cut cross-country, and though I didn't arrive in time to see the climax of the chase, I saw enough to be able to reconstruct the drama.

Two things saved Vic's life, or at least kept his hide unperforated. The first was the levee for being there, and the second was the motorcycle for being able to scale it. He reached the levee with the Pontiac hot on his heels, sailed right up to the top, did a flop, left my motorcycle lying on her side gasping for breath, and took off like a scalded cat for the pitch-black labyrinth of barges, hatches, and catwalks.

The Pontiac had obviously made several assaults on the slope: for there was still a dust cloud hanging in the air, like an Indiana dirt track. The car was now parked halfway up the levee with the lights shining almost straight up.

The gentleman who sought satisfaction, honorable or otherwise, was standing on top of the levee, waving his tinplated pistol around, and peering into the black beyond. He'd already fired one shot, but by now Vic was long gone, and the man wasn't about to head into the ambush country where he was hiding, pistol or no pistol. He just stalked about, shouting vituperation into the night, including the good advice that Vic had better keep his Cajun ass down on the levee for a good long time to come.

Then he spotted ol' Paint lying there well-nigh wind-broke, and that ornery cuss went up and shot her about five times, thinking, no doubt, that she was Vic's motorcycle.

That sure made me mad, and I was about to wreak a little vengeance of my own, when I suddenly remembered seeing six-shooters in the movies shoot eight or nine times. I didn't know but what our man might have one of those kind of repeaters. So I maintained my low profile on the ground and waited for the cops, who were not long in coming.

They took the motorcycle assassin into custody, took my statement, and took their leave. Blessed calm settled once again on the riverbank.

I examined ol' Paint, and her wounds turned out not to be fatal: a slug through the back tire and another in the headlight. So I wheeled her over to the trailer and shouted out, "Vic, if you can hear me, better stay wherever you are. That feller is still prowling around the other side of the levee with iron in his fist and fire in his eyes." Then I went to bed.

I suspect it got kind of cold out there on those barges that night.

Drown and Out in New Orleans

It was a cold, bright midwinter day. I was alone on the *Vulcan*. Bound for drydock to have a propeller changed, I was in the middle of the wide Mississippi. A bridge above me solid with a thousand cars stalled in the 4:00 P.M. traffic. A tug and barge fleet lined the shore to starboard, 191 feet of water flowed under me, a banana boat discharged cargo to port at Poydras Street Wharf, and the Algiers ferry was crossing my path dead ahead. Tourists lined the public landing at Canal Street, waiting to board the excursion steamer *President*.

The collision was a muted, submarine rending of steel. The victim—the boat my son and I had built together—stopped, convulsed, and staggered on. The submerged assassin was probably a partially sunken dredge pontoon or small work barge released on an unsuspecting maritime world by Hurricane Betsy. We hit whatever it was in sight of our destination, and had the wound not been mortal, we might have made it to shore safely. But the wound was mortal, and like the man who is visited by violent death, the boat's first reaction was partial paralysis and loss of motor coordination. In striking and then sliding over the obstruction, one propeller was halted in midrevolution, and the engine was killed. The steering levers in the pilothouse were unceremoniously jerked from my hands as the rudders were slammed over and jammed hard starboard, and the boat, crippled and leaderless, began to run in a frenzied circle.

I flew from the pilothouse with sick anxiety, not over the impending death of this boat (for I did not then suspect that she was dying) but rather over the extent of the damage and the fact that I was responsible for her medical bills, and my sure knowledge that if they were extensive I did not have the money to pay them.

Rushing to the stern with a crowbar, I tried to straighten her rudders, for if I could do that, I might still get her to the dock on the remaining engine. It was so near, but now all of a sudden so far. I strained and strained. The crowbar bent. The rudders did not budge. The radio and the salvage vessel it would fetch now seemed my only alternative. But then I remembered: there was, for the moment, no radio. For I did not then have the $118 needed to redeem it from the repair shop.

I started back to the pilothouse, for there was always the whistle. Someone would hear the strident blasts and know that something other

A harbor tug similar to the *Vulcan*

than sheer good spirits motivated them. I passed the engine room and glanced in. "Oh, God," I said aloud. "She's gone!" Both engines were partially submerged—this could only mean a gaping wound in her hull. I must get off and away from her. Nothing more could be done. The front deck was already awash, ankle deep. She was sinking fast.

Everything I owned and held dear was on that boat: my books, tools, clothes, records, letters from home, pictures, personal documents—everything but the house that sheltered my family back in Cincinnati (and I did not own much of that). How to save all this? I could not. It was soon to disappear forever. All I could save at the moment was myself.

I was aware as I donned my orange life jacket of the drama and uniqueness of what was happening to me, and that I must abandon ship with dignity and by all means keep a firm hold on my glasses. They were my only pair. Then, promptly forgetting both resolves, I splashed my way to the starboard side of the front deck, did an almost military about-face to port, and took off running. Slowed by water now well above my ankles, I reached the port side, grabbed my nose, and leaped. And landed all of a foot away—without the spectacles. I have no idea why I jumped—it was totally irrational; I could have merely stepped off the boat and swum away—but I did leap, and there now reside, 191 feet down, not only the rusted bones of my beloved boat but a pair of eyeglasses that would reveal that their owner was more than a little nearsighted.

Swimming away, I turned and sadly watched the death throes of the fine vessel that my son and I had spent an agonizingly cold winter and thousands of hours in building. Though she was only a small, twin-screw diesel tug, she had proved to be a good one and had traveled many miles of waterway in her short but active life.

She went with dignity, just as a boat should. Her last moments were as impressive as any queen of the high seas who decides in mid-ocean that it is time to die. First, down by the head, then her stern reared straight up. One of her gleaming bronze propellers was still slowly revolving a final farewell. And the drops of water flung from the blades caught and held the sun like small jewels. She plunged then like a sounding, stricken whale for the bottom.

Just before she disappeared forever beneath the surface, air trapped and compressed in her vitals proved too much for her windows. "She blows," I thought, echoing the eternal cry of the whaler's lookout as the windows blew out simultaneously in a spectacular shower of glass and water that also caught its share of the sun's rays and prismed and coruscated the light in a final brilliant farewell. Then she was gone, and a great part of my life was gone. There was not even an oil slick recognizable as hers among the many to mark the place of her passing. If I were to follow her, there would be even less to mark my passing and far less attendant dignity, for I would fight to the very end.

No river in the world is as wide as the Mississippi when viewed from eight inches above the surface. So vast is it that one fancies a crown or curvature can be seen in the center. This was less pronounced for me because I was near that center, but it was a long way to either bank. The slackest water, though, was to be found opposite New Orleans, and that is the way I struck out. I was not yet afraid and not yet uncomfortable.

But I soon discovered two dangers. The first was that even moderately cold water will soon drain your energy faster than adrenalin can replace it, and the second was that you cannot swim in a life preserver. I was making for the far shore for all I was worth, but at the rate I was going I would be in the Gulf of Mexico before I reached land and be dead of exposure long before I got there. I was afraid now for the first time. Each kick and splash gained me nothing, and my efforts were getting feebler as cold and numbness took control. My teeth began to chatter; there was no warmth to the sun. The dirty brown water swirled on, carrying me with it. I was surrounded by human activity; I saw people everywhere, yet I was the loneliest man in the world.

Surely some among those thousands of eyes along the shore and on the bridge must realize that this odd playlet was for real and that the actor might actually die. Surely someone in that vast audience must have sense enough to know that there was a man out there who desperately needed help. I had been in the water for nearly half an hour. I was numb with cold and very afraid. I had faced death before, but it had promised to be swift. This was not going to be that way. This was going to be ugly, slow, and unpleasant, and I would be dragged kicking and squalling every step of the way.

Then came the reprieve. Twin bursts of black smoke erupted from the stacks of a tug. I was to be saved, but I had had a right to be afraid. I was glad that I would be saved before undignified panic took control. During whatever was left of my life, I could look back on this experience and say that the bony hand did not have to seize me by the scruff of the neck, the sepulchral voice did not have to admonish me, "Here, here now. Come along quietly like a man." I had been prepared, I could tell myself, to march off nobly by his side.

But the angel of reprieve became instead an engine of terror. Her lines were thrown off and she darted from the landing, sniffing hither and yon like a coursing terrier. Apparently her pilot had not witnessed the sinking but had only been told that it had happened. He charged heroically and recklessly to the scene, searching for waters dotted with bobbing heads or crowded life rafts filled with grateful survivors. I am sure it never occurred to him that the object of his efforts was only one cold, frightened man heading reluctantly for the Gulf of Mexico.

As the rescue boat drew nearer, still in its mad helter-skelter, I recognized her as the *Tuscaloosa*, a tug I knew well. The pilot searched the vast river; the deckhand on the bow below searched the near surface. So diligently did this noble Cajun search—leaning forward, foot on towing bitt, eyes shaded by hand from the sun, so Deerslayer-like—that he failed to see me. Yet we were on a collision course. I was shouting at the top of my lungs, leaping from the water like an orange porpoise and waving my arms in frantic semaphore. By now I was not trying to attract attention to be rescued but only trying to be saved from my saviors.

The boat drew nearer, but the Cajun saw me not. It was getting closer, closer, still fixed upon me. I would like to say that in this final moment I resigned myself and if only by God was heard to mutter, "Well, this sure promises to be swift and that was what I wanted." But I did not. I just kept yelling with increasingly less dignity. I had let myself down at the end. The bow was nearly upon me. It would soon be over.

Only in the proverbial nick of time did the deckhand deign to glance down and, lo and behold, there floated the loudly hollering, wildly gesticulating object of his search. He communicated this surprising fact to the pilot, again just in the nick of time. The boat sheered off, practically drowning me in the bow wash. Then it circled and effected my rescue.

Once on deck, I began to shiver and my teeth chattered uncontrollably until I thought, as Homer would put it, that my limbs would become unstrung and darkness cloud my eyes. This reaction was due not to fear and relief, mind you, but simply to the chill that had seeped into the innermost man. There was no reserve of calories to stoke up the fires. I would have to be rekindled. And I was. The crew put me in a hot shower and kept me there twenty minutes until I could once again stand still and I had begun to talk.

My first act was to call the landing and arrange for a friend to pick me up, and while I waited I thanked those fellows until they were embarrassed. I was dressed in some oversized but dry clothes that belonged to a crew member, and upon arriving back at East Bank Marine Service I called—in this order—my insurance company, my wife, the Coast Guard, and the Corps of Engineers.

On hearing the news, my wife began to cry, not because of *our* losing the boat, for she hated it, but for *my* losing the boat, for she knew I loved it. Apparently my son was lurking in the background because she murmured something to someone, and the ether was filled with loud blubberings. For Jimmy too had loved the boat, had worked as hard as any man in helping to build it on that cold and wintry alluvial plain where she was born. Already a full-blooded riverman at fifteen, he had looked forward to joining me soon in New Orleans.

I do not know whether my insurance man cried. If he did, he was at least manly enough to wait until we hung up. The mortgage-holding banks for sure didn't shed any tears. They let the insurance man do it for them. The Coast Guard was brusque and mostly uninterested: the boat was in 191 feet of water, no hands went with her, she damaged no other vessel in her dying, and she presented no marine hazard. Her name was stricken from the rolls of the United States Merchant Marine.

The Corps of Engineers office, concerned only with its responsibility for keeping the river open for navigation, was businesslike. They duly noted the *Vulcan*'s passing and the following day, in the classic manner of the bureaucracy, sent me a telegram instructing me to place a buoy on the boat and informing me that if I didn't I would be responsible for any accidents caused by her lonely presence a couple of hundred feet down. I decided to take my chances that no submarine would be nosing around down there and that if anything else hit her it was due to join her. No, she would have to do without a tethered memorial. Even if a submarine ever did hit her, he would be hard pressed to identify the object of his problem. This stretch of the Mississippi is America's own "Iron Bottom Bay," littered with the corpses of tugs, barges, ships, and dry-docks, all victims of one another or of some hurricane.

I fooled around New Orleans for a while, directionless and in shock, like a cowboy who has lost his faithful horse. I was waiting for the insurance company to earn all those hard-earned dollars I'd paid to it. Soon it did, and when the smoke of fast-closing creditors cleared, I had $1,200 to show for two years of the hardest work I had ever done. This was my grubstake for the next phase of my life.

Epilogue

After the *Vulcan* sank, I was left in a kind of limbo. I had some excellent job offers in New Orleans, but my family was in Cincinnati. It was hard to have put all the time and effort I had invested in New Orleans and not have it exert a pull on me, but I wanted to go back where I belonged. I considered staying and working as a marine insurance adjuster but totally rejected the offer to do fleet repair. I had spent too many days welding in the bowels of a barge when the outside temperature was 105 and Lord knows what it was inside with the Louisiana sun beating down on the steel decks. Even locally born workers regularly passed out doing this work and had to be carried from the innards of barges. I had even heard of a few who had died.

As I hung around debating the future, New Orleans began to seem more and more like a foreign country to me. Going there was a grand adventure and the city was fascinating, but it would never be home. Anyway, I had long dreamed of building a houseboat big enough for a family to live on. And I hadn't seen the green hills and valleys of Ohio for too long a time.

I loaded all my equipment and possessions aboard the old Plymouth sedan I had converted into a sort of pickup truck, sold my motorcycle, enjoyed one more night out with Vic, and headed for Cincinnati.

I realized as I drove north how eager I was to get back to my beautiful, familiar, serene Ohio River, with her tree-clad hills, her glorious sunsets, the long evening shadows cast across her placid waters.

I got my first glimpse of her beauty at Paducah, and it was like coming home from the war. The best was yet to come. The farther I proceeded eastward upriver across northern Kentucky, the lovelier the old Ohio looked. Cottonwoods and willows lined her banks, and the hills became steeper. I had not even known how much I missed this ladylike stream.

Once home, I settled in and reacquainted myself with my family. They were a truly generous bunch and welcomed me with festivities— if not of the fatted calf variety at least of the pork chops and fried potatoes type. I went back to the civilized towboating of the Ohio River, and I eventually built that houseboat. I worked many more years in the place I loved best.

As I visit the Ohio River today and think back on our years together,

I know that nothing will ever be quite the same as it was when I plied her waters: there are more power plants, newer and even larger lock and dam systems, and more rules and regulations, fines, and legal procedures that have to take some of the fun out of piloting. But I know the people have not changed: the crew on the huge towboat I see stretched out along the water is still a family as they plow along for a month's duty. They are like me and my old friends; they have the same problems and worries and joys, the same risks and rewards.

I think of how much the river has taken from me, and how much it has given. I wouldn't trade my life and adventures with anyone. Looking back, I think there were more ups than downs. It must not have looked like too bad a life, for my son, Captain James H. Coomer IV, is carrying on the riverboat tradition begun by my grandfather, the old marshal of Burnside, those many years ago.

Glossary

"all gone": signal phrase meaning that all lines securing a boat, barge, or tow have been removed and that the vessel is free to get under way. Unfortunately, when a green deckhand signals "all gone," he may be stating the literal truth—not only has he released the barges to be removed from the fleet but somehow the rest of the fleet as well! You and your barges start up the river, the balance of the fleet starts down. Such an occurrence is usually accompanied by much swearing from the pilot and always by much extra work for all.

"all stop": signal phrase meaning to place throttles in neutral position. The tow will still be moving under its own momentum.

ass: a quadruped and a much-discussed part of human anatomy; also a term applied to unusually long and heavy boats that can control a big tow in tight situations such as making locks or navigating sharp bends. A boat that backs (moves astern) well.

barges: large, non–self-propelled cargo carriers of many types—open hoppers, covered hoppers, tank barges, etc. They can carry from 1,500 to 3,000 tons of cargo.

bitts: *See* timberheads.

bow: the front of a vessel.

bullnose: rounded end of the outer guide wall and inner guide wall that separates the two lock chambers. They are rounded so that in a collision a tow will tend to carom off instead of hitting head-on; they are painted silver with black diagonal stripes.

buoys: green buoys are painted green, shaped like a tin can, and called "cans"; red buoys are painted red, pointed at the top, and called "nuns," for no reason that I have ever heard. They are floating devices placed by the Coast Guard to mark underwater hazards such as sandbars, rocks, dikes, and to indicate the "sailing line." If you are a boater and not overly good at memorizing things you could post at your pilot station a sign that reads "Red Right Returning." This means that if you are going upstream, you keep the red nuns to your starboard or right side. If you have trouble with port and starboard, paint one wall red and the other green.

bumpers: large bundles of interwoven old lashings used to fend the tow off lock walls, thus prohibiting sparks. Sometimes called "possums."

captain: chief executive responsible for the overall management and safe navigation of the tow. Like most people, captains come in two varieties—good and bad. A bad one exercises too much mouth, too few standards, and the wrong kind of authority, and the boat shows it. The captain stands two six-hour steering watches, traditionally the forward watch—that is, from 6:00 A.M. to noon and from 6:00 P.M. to midnight. He keeps the boat's log and books and can fire personnel. *See also* pilot

cargo: material carried in barges

cavels: double-horned deck hardware securely welded on barges for the purpose of securing wires or lashings. *See also* timberheads

cheater bar: a six-foot length of pipe that is placed over the handle of a ratchet to give extra leverage for tightening the tow wires.

company notch: throttles in full-ahead position on both engines for maximum speed.

cook: an invaluable member of the crew, not only for nutrition but for morale. Cooks may be male or female. They must turn out three hearty, attractive meals a day, plus plenty of cakes and pies for snacks, since food is one of the few pleasures on a thirty-day stretch.

cowboy: an unwise pilot who sometimes pulls off amazing maneuvers and is consequently held in high regard by crew members and other pilots and captains but who is, like other boat handlers, subject to licensing by the Coast Guard, which can unlicense him when feats of derring do fail to come off safely.

deadman: a massive block of concrete buried in a riverbank with mooring rings embedded in the top to hold fleets of barges.

deckhand: Crew member whose duties consist of putting the tow together with tow wires, guiding the helmsman through locks, and assisting with the delivery of barges up and down the river, as well as cleaning, painting, and general maintenance of boats and barges. The work can be hazardous when a deckhand must walk the long dark tow at night or in winter when the beast can be iced over and slippery.

dispatcher: one who radios the towboat and issues orders on which barges are to be added to which tows. Often the bane of a riverman's life, they spend time in offices arranging—in total disarray—toy barges that represent their 195-foot counterparts.

downbound: headed downstream, toward Cairo and New Orleans. *See also* oxbow

draft: the distance from the lowest point of a full barge to the water's surface, or how deep in the water any vessel rides, generally nine feet for a load and eighteen inches for an empty.

engineer: one in charge of the engine room, called the chief, who starts and stops the engines on orders from the captain or pilot, maintains all mechanical appliances and appurtenances of the vessel, including the washing machine and the toaster as well as the engines. They tend to guard their domains like grumpy old St. Bernards and, if put upon, can be as temperamental as ballet dancers but if not riled are generally the most placid of all crew members. Even the most ferocious captain treads lightly in the presence of a grizzled old engineer; after all, the chief knows how to start the engines and check the oil, which most captains do not.

face wires: heavy steel cables that affix the boat to the tow, tensioned by face wire winches on the bow of the boat. They have been known to break in a hard down steer; when they do, the boat goes one way and the barges another.

facing down: the approach of a boat to a barge or a tow in the downstream direction, less controlled than facing up and, if done badly, accompanied by the sound of sleeping bodies hitting the floor.

facing up: the approach of a boat to a barge or a tow in the upstream direction, a gentle easing of the towing knees of the boat against the barge followed by the placing and tightening of the face wires.

flanking: a truly amazing ability of a modern American river towboat; generally employed in a downstream situation, accomplished by the experienced manipulation of all rudders and the use of the power and thrust of the wheels, by which a tow is moved sideways through the water without gaining or losing ground fore or aft in situations in which it is impossible to steer around a severe bend. Needless to say, if you run out of river width before you run out of the bend, you have some problems, like gathering up the bits and pieces of a twenty-barge tow. A wise pilot and not a cowboy will slow his tow to a manageable speed, keep the engines in reverse, use the flanking rudders, and accomplish a controlled float around the bend.

flanking or backing rudders: a pair of rudders located ahead of each propeller, used when the boat is backing and the wheelwash is directed toward the bow of the vessel.

fleet: *See* tow

freeboard: the distance from the water's surface to the main deck. If the draft is ever such that there is no freeboard and your feet are wet, you had best abandon ship!

"full ahead": signal phrase, sometimes known as the "company notch," meaning to give her all she's got.

guard: a walkway along each side of the main deck superstructure of a towboat or barge.

hard down: pushing the steering levers as far to the port or the starboard as they will go, named so because of the tendency to keep pushing on the levers as hard as you can in order to get an extra degree of rudder angle that will allow you to make the bend, even after you have experienced a sinking feeling that you will not.

head: the point on the barges farthest from the boat (about 1,000 feet for a full tow). Also, a toilet.

headboat: an unpowered, permanently moored vessel retired from active service, such as an old barge, towboat, or steamboat, which may become a mooring vessel for barge fleets, or may have floats attached to make a yacht club.

"kill 'er out": signal phrase meaning to apply sufficient power in reverse to stop the tow.

lashing or grass lines: working lines, usually one and a half to three inches in diameter, now of manmade materials but formerly of natural fibers such as manila or hemp, which are seldom used today because they are subject to rot and freezing and lack the strength of the newer poly lines. Plastic lines have one drawback—if they break under strain they can snap back and kill or badly injure anyone in the way. To a green hand, lines seem to have a life of their own, and he may find himself impersonating Laocoon. (By the way, there are no "ropes" on a towboat.)

line-haul tow: a full tow, fifteen to twenty-five barges, all in one tow and going to the same location, pushed by one big towboat. The boat delivers or adds barges on its long trip but basically it is the same tow that departed perhaps from Cairo on its way to Pittsburgh. It may be served by tugs when necessary.

lite boat or loose-headed: a towboat being navigated without barges, which is difficult to keep on straight course and under the application of too much power tends to dive and run the bow under water. A pilot who persists in applying power will wash all the equipment off the front deck and be roundly cursed by the mate, not to mention the company that owns the boat.

mate: a crewman who oversees the deck crew in their duties, in particular in assembling the tow, and teaches them the crafts of making and lassoing cavels; he is also invaluable to the pilot in a tough lockage or landing.

navigation light: one of the hundreds of lights installed along the banks of the inland waterways and maintained by the Coast Guard. Each light post serves as a mile post, and the lights may be Fixed Green, Fixed Red, Flashing Green, Flashing Red, Fixed White, Flashing White, Occulting White—each with its own pattern of flashes. They theoretically guide a mariner around the bends in the river, but I prefer to rely on my eyes, my knowledge of the river, and my radar.

one whistle, two whistle: *See* overtaking *and* passing

overtaking, one-whistle: an audible signal blown when the intention is to overtake and pass a vessel on your port side, passing on its starboard side.

overtaking, two-whistle: an audible signal blown when the intention is to overtake and pass a vessel on your starboard side, passing on its port side.

oxbow: places on the river where a boat is traveling due north while also downbound.

passing, one-whistle: audible signal blown to indicate that two vessels approaching head to head will pass each other port to port.

passing, two-whistle: audible signal blown to indicate that vessels approaching head to head will pass each other starboard to starboard. The upbound vessel blows first, but the downbound vessel has the right of way and may disagree. If so, he blows a danger signal of four or more blasts, then indicates by the one- or two-whistle signal which side of the river he prefers. Nowadays, most of this is decided by radio, often before the boats even come within sight of one another.

pilot: officer who, with the captain, shares the duty of steering the boat, stands the after watch—that is, from noon to 6:00 P.M. and from midnight to 6:00 A.M. Pilots sometimes labor under the opinion that they should be captains and often act as father confessor to the crew, who are usually outraged about something.

pilothouse: the highest elevation on a towboat and the place from which it is steered. If you ask pilothouse personnel, they will say that it is where the brains of the vessel reside; if you ask the deck crew, you may get another answer.

pleasure boats: small creatures skittering around the surface of most inland waterways, especially in summer. They love to pull out in front of a big tow, not seeming to realize that this behemoth cannot stop on a dime. Every year a few are run down and people killed by their careless operation. Unfortunately, you do not have to pass a driver's test to buy and run one.

port: the left side of a vessel as you face forward.

possum: *See* bumpers

radar: an acronym for Radio Detection and Ranging, an electronic miracle developed by the British in World War II and since installed on towboats. A modern person who trusts technology can run a 1,200-foot tow in fog so thick it obscures the handrails around the pilothouse; those who don't believe will head for the bank and "catch a willer tree" (tie off) when the pilothouse gets too spooky and the river even more so.

rake ends: bow end of jumbo barge (195 feet by 35 feet) that has a long upslope from waterline to deck level. The other end is generally square. These barges are called semi-integrated, and on the Ohio, a maximum tow of them is fifteen, creating a tow 975 feet long by 105 feet wide, to fit in a lock chamber 1,200 by 110 feet.

ratchet: a large, heavy piece of equipment with a central barrel with internal threading and a long, externally threaded rod on each end, used for tightening the steel cables that hold a tow together. The weight of the tool and the necessity of using dozens of them all over a 1,000-foot tow requires a crew with plenty of muscle. *See also* cheater bar

river navigation: moving from point A to point B without getting lost or stopping at Cincinnati to ask directions to Pittsburgh, usually no problem because detailed charts are available and both banks can be seen. (I know one pilot, however, who missed the mouth of the Cumberland River and was busily heading into the Tennessee before the cook pointed out his mistake.)

"roll 'er back": signal phrase meaning that pilot has put the throttles in reverse and thus commenced stopping the tow. Indicated by the mate at the head of the tow facing the pilothouse and waving his arms in that direction; the more agitated his movements, the harder the pilot backs. If he becomes *very* agitated, it indicates two things: that he wants this mess stopped as quickly as possible and that he is busily figuring out how to blame the impending disaster on the pilot. If he takes off running down the tow, the pilot may as well kill himself.

starboard: the right side of a vessel as you face forward.

steering levers: steel levers, sometimes called "sticks," which activate the hydraulic system that moves the rudders (modern towboats are not guided with old-time steering wheels). The upper, shorter levers control the flanking rudders; the longer, lower ones control the steering rudders. When the boat is on straight rudder, the levers are in fore and aft alignment with the vessel; the rudders are always at the same angle as the levers. This is called a "follow-up" system. To steer to port, for example, one pushes the steering lever to port.

steering rudders: rudders located behind the propeller being used when the boat is moving ahead and the wheelwash is directed astern.

timberheads, cavels, bitts: solidly affixed steel devices on boats and barges used to secure lines and cables.

stern: the rear of a vessel.

toothpick: a steel rod used in tightening ratchets, which has also been known to serve as the last word in a personal dispute.

tow: the completed assemblage of barges, wired together and including a towboat. A tow is tightly cabled together so that it becomes a single unit. For barges to become a tow, they must have a boat; without a boat, a group of barges is a fleet, which is securely tied off to a shore facility— or had better be!

towboat: the powered prime mover of river freight with all the necessary equipment to assemble a tow of barges and navigate them. It also contains a galley and living quarters for the crew and an engine room for the huge diesel engines.

towing knees: stiffly braced steel structures resembling drawn-up human knees that are located on the bow of a towboat or tug and butt up to the barges. I have seen tow knees bent back, knocked flat, and knocked off by careless pilots.

tug: a small towboat with 400 to 1,000 horsepower. The switch-engines of the industry, they assist larger tows in landing and delivering barges, crew members, visitors, or even groceries to the big towboats. A tug is the place to learn what boat handling is all about.

under the point: like almost anything else that moves in occasional curves, water is subject to centrifugal force. In swift current conditions, as a boat sweeps around a bend the greater volume and velocity will be at the outside perimeter. The short side of the bend is "the point," thus the current "under the point" may be moving several miles per hour less than that in mid-river or on the far side.

upbound: heading upstream; on the Ohio River, this means traveling toward Pittsburgh.

up the hill: leaving a vessel before the days of duty are completed. For example, a disgruntled deckhand is heard to say, "Fuck this lashup, I'm goin' up the hill," which means he quits; some have quit so suddenly that they have swum ashore. Or, a disgruntled captain says to a deckhand, "Pack yore bags and git yore ass up the hill," which means he's fired; this has happened with such dispatch that the newly unemployed crewman finds himself with bag in hand at 2:00 A.M. on a dark and wintry night in Stringtown Fly, a place I defy the Census Bureau or Greyhound to locate.

utter confusion: a series of signals, familiar to all pilots, given by deckhands who absolutely don't know what they are doing. Of course, *they* know what they want; it is the idiot pilot who is confused.

valley square: a highly specialized barge developed by the Mississippi Valley Barge Line. No longer in active use, they were 150 by 35 feet and had a deckhouse on top of the hull that measured 100 by 30 by 9 feet. The deckhouse had sliding doors and was decked inside so that the barge could carry cargo in the lower hold and at deck level. They were used for cargo that had to be kept dry in inclement weather, such as sugar in bags, tin plate drums of various products, and boxed goods like cyanide, antifreeze, etc. Now retired, they serve as headboats for marinas, floating restaurants, and mooring barges for barge fleets.

wheel: the propeller; most towboats have two, one for each engine. They may vary in diameter from three to twelve feet and may be surrounded by a steel shroud called a "Kort Knozzle," said to increase horsepower by 25 percent; otherwise the vessel is referred to as an "open-wheeled boat."

wire: strong, one-inch diameter steel cables used for fastening barges together and the boat to the barges.

Lake Michigan

DATE DUE

WITHDRAWN

INDIANA

ILLIN

Mississippi

Illinois

River

Fork

West

East Fork

Mad

River White River

Wabash River

Tobacco Patch Light

Evansville

River

MISSOURI

River

Ohio

Green

River

Tennessee

Cumberland

MEDIA CENTER
ELIZABETHTOWN COMMUNITY COLLEGE
600 COLLEGE STREET ROAD
ELIZABETHTOWN, KY 42701

River

TENNESSE

jmh